D0065785

Cold
Winds,
Warm
Winds

Also by Judith Shapiro and Liang Heng
Son of the Revolution
After the Nightmare

Judith Shapiro and
Liang Heng

Cold Winds, Warm Winds

Intellectual Life in China Today

Wesleyan University Press
Middletown, Connecticut

Library of Congress Cataloging-in-Publication Data

Shapiro, Judith, 1953–
Cold winds, warm winds.

(Wesleyan paperback)
Bibliography: p.
Includes index.
    1. China—Intellectual life—1976– . 2. China—
Politics and government—1976 . I. Liang, Heng.
II. Title.
DS779.23.S525 1986   951.05'8   85-29513
ISBN 0-8195-5162-7 (alk. paper)
ISBN 0-8195-6168-1 (pbk. : alk. paper)

We would like to express our gratitude to the Asia Watch Committee of the Fund for Free Expression for its support of this project, and to Aryeh Neier in particular, who suggested it and saw it through, and to Sophie Silberberg, who contributed to it in many unexpected and gratefully received ways.

All inquiries and permissions requests should be addressed to the Publisher, Wesleyan University Press, 110 Mt. Vernon Street, Middletown, Connecticut 06457.

Distributed by Harper & Row Publishers, Keystone Industrial Park, Scranton, Pennsylvania 18512.

Manufactured in the United States of America
First Edition

Contents

Foreword

A central question for our times is whether a contemporary totalitarian state is capable of transforming itself. Is it possible for a free society to emerge, by either evolution or revolution, after all independent institutions and associations have been destroyed, and after a twentieth-century totalitarian state's mechanisms of surveillance and control have been put firmly in place?

Judith Shapiro and Liang Heng's richly detailed account of the emergence of a measure of intellectual freedom in China after the long night of the Cultural Revolution is an extraordinarily valuable contribution to the literature about totalitarianism. In writing about the rebirth of a degree of free expression, they are exploring territory that is largely uncharted and, though they cannot predict what they will eventually find in the China that is changing as they write, to read their account is to share in the excitement and pleasure of discovery.

The territory they are exploring is uncharted because, in the little more than half a century since Stalin consolidated power in the Soviet Union and Hitler came to power in Germany, totalitarianism has not been lastingly rolled back anywhere except by military defeat by external forces. In that period, half of the world's population has come under totalitarian rule. Of course, Hungary seemed to be transforming itself in 1956; Czechoslovakia in 1968; and Poland in 1981. In each instance, however, the movements for freedom within those countries were crushed: by direct Soviet military intervention in the case of Hungary and Czechoslovakia, and by the Polish army acting in place of the Red Army to dismantle Solidarity. We never got a chance to discover how the state might have been changed if the movements that inspired those military coups had been permitted to continue and to develop.

One of the many differences between what is happening in the China described by Judith Shapiro and Liang Heng and what happened in Hungary, Czechoslovakia, and Poland is that the movement for intellectual freedom in China does not imminently threaten the Communist Party's monopoly of state power. In that respect, it resembles movements that are currently underway in several countries of post-Solidarity Eastern Europe (or Central Europe, as some—including Milan Kundera—prefer to call the region). What happened to Solidarity signaled the futility, at least for many years to come, of efforts in Eastern Europe to take over the machinery and functions of the state, or to share power with the state, or to negotiate with the state over the use of its power. As a consequence, those concerned with freedom in Eastern Europe have now turned in a different direction.

To a reader of Judith Shapiro and Liang Heng's book on the recent history of intellectual freedom in China who, like me, approaches the subject with more awareness of what is going on today in Eastern Europe, this question of differences and similarities is particularly fascinating. A starting point in listing differences might be the metaphor expressed in the title, *Cold Winds, Warm Winds*. It signifies intervention from on high to alter the climate. Shapiro and Liang persuade me that this is appropriate in the case of China, but it would be wholly out of place in describing the current efforts to promote intellectual freedom in Poland, Czechoslovakia, Hungary, and Yugoslavia.

In those four countries of Eastern Europe, state authorities have done nothing to encourage the development of a freer society, and intellectuals are not now focusing their energies on efforts to get the state to permit a wider latitude for expression. Instead, many Poles and other East Europeans are attempting to ignore the state and to exercise intellectual freedom by creating an alternative culture, which exists alongside the official culture. It is in Poland that this alternative culture has developed most remarkably. Four years after martial law was imposed, more than five hundred underground periodicals—from one-page factory news sheets to book-sized scholarly quarterlies—are published regularly. One weekly has a circulation of fifty thousand and many times that number of readers. Hundreds of books are published underground annually in quantities that would seem respectable to trade-book publishers in the United States and in editions that are sometimes superior in format to those published officially in Poland. And, literally hundreds of thousands of Poles take part in alternative education programs, living-room theater, dance, musical performances, and art exhibits. Elsewhere in Eastern Europe, alternative cultural life is not so well developed as in Poland. Even in severely repressive Czechoslovakia, however—where prison sentences and psychiatric confinement of dissidents are nearly as harsh as in the Soviet Union— approximately a hundred books are published annually by intrepid underground publishers. And there, as well as in Poland, Hungary, and Yugoslavia, serious work in literature and art is identified to a significantly greater extent with the alternative culture than with the culture of the state.

Though intervention from on high as been essential in

China, Shapiro and Liang make it clear that what is taking place today is also dependent on many other forces. The richness of their work comes from their close reading of Chinese literature and political writing and their astute observation of the performing arts and the mass media. Through their descriptions and analyses, deeply informed by their knowledge of Chinese history, culture, and custom, they present a compelling portrait of writers and artists at work in a society in which the limits on expression are expanding but also undergo unforeseeable, and dangerous, contractions. Shapiro and Liang enable us to see how considerations of personal advancement and enrichment, the desire to get a work approved for publication or presentation, and concerns about artistic integrity and excellence are all caught up in and contribute to the emergence of some measure of intellectual freedom.

To a far greater extent than in Eastern Europe, of course, China's movement toward freer expression is dependent on forces that emanate from within. Size, geography, history, and language are all obvious factors in making developments in China less susceptible to external influence. Yet Shapiro and Liang, whose own marriage reflects the increased contact between China and the West since the end of the Cultural Revolution, are particularly sensitive to the impact of the opening to Western ideas upon China and to the ways in which Chinese react to those ideas. They also write with an awareness of how China's eagerness for material advancement and economic ties to the West influences its leaders to permit a wider opening for Western ideas.

An especially important force in Eastern Europe is nationalism. Anti-Soviet nationalism is a force in Poland, Czechoslovakia, and Hungary; and, in a somewhat different manner, the nationalism of Serbs, Croats, Slovenes, and the other ethnic and linguistic groups that make up Yugoslavia is a dynamic influence in that country. Its effect on movements for intellectual freedom is manifest in the concern with history and language, and in the rediscovery of folk literature and customs that is a focus of much scholarly effort in those countries. Until reading Shapiro and Liang, I had not understood that nationalism is also a factor in the movement for intellectual freedom in China. It is not, of course, nationalism that is based on resentment against subjugation by an external power, as in Eastern Europe. Rather, it reflects the fear of writers and artists that their long subjugation to their own state has rendered them incapable of producing Chinese literature and art that is of international significance. Their struggle to create work that matters artistically is a way of trying to reclaim their national heritage.

For a reader of Judith Shapiro and Liang Heng less preoccupied with the similarities and dissimilarities to another part of the world, *Cold Winds, Warm Winds* will inspire quite different reflections. What I expect that every reader will find, however, is that this book is both a joy to read and a major contribution to thinking about reclaiming freedom from total tyranny.

Aryeh Neier

Prologue

Many of the experiments that have taken place in China under the leadership of Deng Xiaoping are widely known and discussed in the West. Tales of peasant entrepreneurs running chicken farms and buying color TVs have become familiar. But less well known are the implications of the changes in economic policy for intellectual life. How have they altered the way people think, speak, relate to one another, create, and learn? How have they affected values and self-perceptions?

This book is based on two studies of the climate of intellectual freedom in China that we made for the Asia Watch Committee of the Fund for Free Expression. The first was written when the autumn 1983 campaign against "spiritual pollution" had just ended, and Chinese intellectuals in China and abroad were alarmed to see what appeared to be an upsurge of the dogmatic leftism of the Mao era. It seemed that it was still very easy to set off a Cultural Revolution–style movement, and that much less had been learned from that ten-year tragedy than many had hoped. Sudden political shifts have been characteristic of Chinese life since the Communist victory in 1949, but this short campaign was an extreme and disturbing example, especially because, since the death of Mao, China had gradually, if unevenly, been becoming a more open society.

Intellectual freedom is a massive subject, encompassing, in the case of China, matters as disparate as creative integrity, friendship with foreigners, and political study meetings. Our first report, written in the shadow of the campaign against spiritual pollution and intended primarily as a study of it, focused on how the campaign affected freedom of belief, speech, artistic creation, and information. We also included an overview of the major changes in the climate of intellectual freedom since the death of Mao, which has become Part I of this book.

In early 1985 we had the opportunity to return to China for three months. We found one of the freest intellectual climates since before the Cultural Revolution. The negative effects of the campaign against spiritual pollution had been much less long-lasting than we had initially feared, and many campaign victims with whom we spoke had regained their earlier status. As the Chinese metaphor would have it, the "cold winds" of late 1983 were in early 1985 blowing much warmer.

This time, our writing was based not, primarily, on our research into the published debate in the Chinese media but on direct conversations with a wide range of Chinese. We spoke with peasants in poor and in prosperous regions, with workers, artists, writers, journalists, engineers, scientists, students, professors, beggars, shopkeepers, entrepreneurs, top policy makers, and the unemployed. We spoke also with dissidents. We lived, most of the time, as Chinese live, visiting areas few foreigners have seen, traveling in crowded and sometimes dangerous vehicles, staying often in hotels intended for Chinese travelers only.

Many of the people with whom we spoke we had known for years. (One of us, Liang Heng, was born in China and did not leave until 1981; the other, Judith Shapiro, taught there from 1979 to 1981.) Most others also talked to us freely.

China's present official policy of openness to the West permits ordinary people to express their hospitality and curiosity, and indeed Chinese are sometimes more open with outsiders than they can afford to be with each other. For many Chinese, our Sino-American marriage is a symbol of China's opening to the outside world: they treat us more warmly because of it. And foreign friends, like foreign cigarettes and foreign television, have now become a symbol of status.

Another matter to be mentioned at the outset is that some of the values underlying this book, including the assumption that intellectual freedom is a positive thing, are radically different from those espoused by the Chinese Communist party and indeed by large sectors of the Chinese population. Advocates of such notions as "freedom of expression," "human rights," and "artistic freedom" have often been attacked in China as "bourgeois liberals" or "extreme individualists." Those who seek intellectual freedom have been seen as reckless and disruptive, naive about the realities of life and guilty of "bad thought." Furthermore, in a country where 23 percent of the population is illiterate, where only ten years ago knowledge could be extremely dangerous, and where an "intellectual" is a middle-school graduate, even artists and professors can often be far less concerned with intellectual freedom than they are with corruption and abuses of privilege by party leaders, with good work assignments and marriages for their children, and with bettering their living standards. Despite the difficulties in finding a common ground, however, we hope that this book will contribute to mutual understanding by clarifying differences and pointing out areas in which progress has been made.

We have chosen to focus on ordinary citizens rather than the less typical "dissidents," who have received considerable attention elsewhere.[1] When we talk about journalists, we generally refer to people working for official government publications rather than to the editors and writers of the unofficial magazines which flourished briefly from 1978 to 1981 during the Democracy Movement, many of whom have been incarcerated. Furthermore, although an enormous number of arrests and executions were carried out as part of an autumn 1983 crackdown on crime, such important concerns as political imprisonment, violations of due process, and capital punishment are beyond our scope except insofar as they have affected the general climate for intellectual freedom.

Furthermore, despite the improvements we found in early 1985, we remain well aware that China's atmosphere can change radically in a very short time, moving from "tightness" to "looseness," from constraint to liberalization, or vice versa. For this reason we have generally chosen to write in the past tense, although many of our descriptions of the climate and organization of the intellectual life of China continue to hold true as of this writing. Even in the months since early 1985, China has once again become "tighter," although so far nothing approaches in repressiveness the campaign against spiritual pollution. The possibility is nevertheless a real one. China's thousands of years of feudalism have left powerful traditionalist forces, and their periodic recurrence is inevitable, no matter who controls the highest power. A close look at the 1983 campaign may thus, we continue to fear, shed light on the future as well as on the past.

I
Warm Winds, Cold Winds

The Decade of Winter

There has been a tremendous improvement in nearly every aspect of Chinese life since the death of Mao Zedong and the downfall of the ultraleftist "Gang of Four" in 1976. In the decade of the Cultural Revolution (1966–1976) intellectual freedom was virtually nonexistent. The expression of ideological conformity was essential to survival, and political activism virtually the only route to self-advancement. Activism often meant "ferreting out" enemies guilty of crimes of speech and thought. People learned to protect themselves by avoiding friendships and social contacts, maintaining conservatively safe life styles, and hiding their real beliefs and feelings with recitations of the latest political orthodoxies.

There was a sense of nightmarish insanity in much of that era: the entire country's theatrical consumption was restricted to eight "model theatrical picccs"; literature was limited to a blend of revolutionary realism and revolutionary romanticism of the most sterile variety; the political messages of films were their sole messages, and people were forced to attend; libraries were closed, and almost all books not written by Marx, Lenin, or Chairman Mao were burned or locked away; university students were selected on the basis of political attitude and "performance"; intellectuals "stank" and were frequently "persecuted to death"; a misprinted word or a careless phrase could cost a life; husbands, wives, and best friends betrayed one another; letters were opened, and private correspondence addressed abroad was intercepted and used as incriminating evidence; political study meetings were constant, and "criticism/self-criticism" the common agenda; the individual had little value except in the service of the party and state, and love was considered counterrevolutionary; religious expression was suppressed, and monks, imams, priests, and ministers killed, jailed, or sent to the countryside; minority ethnic groups were forbidden to live according to their customs; there was virtually no legal system and no court of appeal; and beatings, torture, induced suicide, and murder, particularly of intellectuals, artists, and high-ranking officials, were routine.

The costs of the Cultural Revolution in actual human life are yet to be measured. There were many ways to die, ranging from execution, suicide, factional warfare, and death by "stray bullet" to illness brought on by life in prison or in the countryside and lack of medical attention. Despite the improvements of recent years, the psychological and economic costs are still being exacted from the Chinese who lived through it. In the cities, they can be counted in lingering material scarcities, unhealed enmities, emotional scars, nightmares, and wasted lives. In some areas of the countryside, they can be seen in the residues of poverty induced by "never forgetting class struggle" and by suppressing essential sideline occupations—such as raising pigs and chickens—as "capitalist."

The worst of the violence was over by 1968, and the Mao cult was deflated with the exposure in 1971 of Minister of Defense Lin Biao, its greatest proponent and Mao's chosen successor, as a "traitor." However, the cold political climate and persecution of intellectuals continued until Mao's death in September 1976 and the ultraleftist clique's downfall two months later.

The greatest protest against the ultraleftists was the Tiananmen Incident on April 5, 1976. Mao was not yet dead and the Gang of Four was still in power. Premier Zhou Enlai, who had been much loved for his attempts to moderate the impact of leftist policies by protecting intellectuals, historic sites, and religious shrines, had died in January of that year. The Gang of Four announced there would be no ceremony to commemorate Zhou on the traditional day for remembrance of the dead. Nevertheless, thousands of people went spontaneously to Beijing's Monument to the Heroes of the Revolution in Tiananmen Square and presented wreaths, put up posters, and read speeches and poems. Many of these were pleas for democracy and an end to imperial-style dictatorship.

The demonstration was suppressed, and, it is said, many people were injured. However, some believe that this pressure from the masses enabled Hua Guofeng and others to "smash" the Gang soon after Mao's death in September and that it paved the way for Deng Xiaoping's return to power (for the second time) in July 1977. Deng immediately did three things: he overturned the "wrong sentences" of the many moderate party leaders who were still in prisons or in the countryside; he reversed the official verdict that the Tiananmen Incident was "counterrevolutionary," thereby signaling support for democracy, protest, and self-expression by the masses; and he began the process of criticizing leftist economic policies and encouraging the development of science, technology, and education.

A Golden Time

Chinese intellectuals often call the years from 1978 to 1980 a "golden time," a time of unprecedented freedom of expression. The Democracy Walls in the major cities were direct successors to the Tiananmen Incident, and they flourished with the blessing of the highest leadership. People could put up posters and cartoons expressing dissatisfaction and advocating whatever they wished. During this period there was an outpouring of demands, from the many thousands of people who had been persecuted, to have their grievances heard. "Rightists," "landlords," "capitalists," "counterrevolutionaries," peasants protesting economic hardships, and "educated youths" who had been sent to the countryside and remote border areas came from all over China to the capital, sometimes traveling thousands of miles without money or train tickets and camping out in the streets. These two movements, the young people's movement for democracy and human rights, and the petitioners' appeals for redress of wrongs, fueled and fed each other: some petitioners put up posters on Democracy Walls, some young people wrote the petitioners' stories in the unofficial publications that burgeoned at the time. Most important, the official party newspapers and radio stations, controlled now by Deng's men, also spoke in support of the people, criticizing the Gang of Four, the Cultural Revolution, and sometimes even the system itself.

The Third Plenary Session of the 11th Central Committee, held at the end of 1978, was an early crystallization of the spirit of that period. Its principal messages were that people should "liberate their thought" from ultraleftist ideology; that they should focus on economic progress by building the Four Modernizations (of agriculture, industry, science and technology, and the military); and that they should criticize the extreme Left. Deng's reform faction triumphed, at least on the top level, over Hua Guofeng's conservative "whateverists" ("Whatever Chairman Mao decided, we must steadfastly support; whatever Chairman Mao directed, we must unhesitatingly carry out"). The Deng group's pragmatic slogan "Practice is the sole criterion for testing truth" echoed Deng's earthier "It doesn't matter if the cat is black or white as long as it catches the rat" and became the hallmark of the new regime.

During that time, many enjoying the warmer winds believed that the degree of liberalization would only increase. They did not understand that Deng needed them to help take power from the "whateverists," and that after his power was consolidated, some liberties would be seen as dispensable, or worse, a threat to the legitimacy of his regime. Just as Mao Zedong had used the masses to help him regain his slipping power during the Cultural Revolution, so Deng Xiaoping was now using them against the leftists; just as Mao had unleashed forces that went beyond his control, so Deng too would quickly feel the need to rein the people back in.

The clamor of discontented voices was indeed overwhelming. The "wrong sentences" handed down by the leftists that needed to be investigated were countless, and the patience Deng asked from the victims was not forthcoming. Anger and disillusionment were often directed not only at the Gang of Four but at the party and even at socialism itself. Dangerous questions were raised about why China was so far behind the Eastern European socialist countries, and, more penetratingly, why it was so backward as compared with capitalist Japan, Taiwan, and Hong Kong. Was China truly socialist, or had the party elite formed a new class of oppressors, creating a new form of alienation of the masses? Hadn't the Gang of Four been carrying out Mao's orders, and if so, shouldn't he be denounced as a red fascist as well?

The screenwriter Bai Hua's *Unrequited Love* (*Ku Lian*) questioned the basic relationship between the people and the party ("You love the motherland, but does the motherland love you?"). A 1979 letter to *China Youth* (*Zhongguo Qingnian*), the Communist Youth League magazine, from a young girl contemplating suicide because she felt that young people, despite the glorious achievements of socialism, had no future, provoked a nationwide debate of overwhelming proportions, and all too many youths concluded that life was indeed meaningless.[1] The journalist-writer Liu Binyan's "Between Men and Demons" (*Ren Yao Zhijian*)[2] dramatized the phenomenal power and corruption of an actual county party secretary. The play by Sha Yexin (among others), *If I Were Real* (*Jiaru Wo Shi Zhende*),[3] described how an ordinary youth impersonated the son of a high party leader and found doors suddenly flung wide, as officials sought to win influence with his purported father. The poet Ye Wenfu wrote "General, You Shouldn't Do That" (*Jiangjun, Bu Neng Zheyang Zuo*),[4] about a man who tore down a kindergarten to build his own fancy living quarters. Meanwhile, the Democracy Wall activists were calling for a Fifth Modernization in politics: democracy.

Writers and artists were producing a flood of the least-restricted work in more than a decade. "Wound" or "scar" literature appeared toward the end of 1977, expressing outrage at the injustice and pain suffered during the Cultural Revolution. By 1979, this was being supplanted by "exposé literature" about the corrupt practices of high party bureaucrats. Love stories could once again be published. Modernistic trends such as stream of consciousness, imagism, and expressionism were explored. The Fourth Congress of Writers and Artists (from October 30 to November 15 of 1979) was a high point of intellectual controversy as young and middle-aged writers from all over China openly criticized the intensely ideological literature of the Cultural Revolution and asserted the importance of the freedom to write without political restrictions; their long-persecuted elders tried to exert a cautioning hand.

In the visual arts, Western influence, especially among oil painters, brought experiments with impressionism, expressionism, neorealism, and even abstract expressionism. Nudes were painted, shocking much of China, especially when they appeared on an often-covered mural in the Beijing airport. Painters' subjects revealed the thoughtful, introspective moods of morally upright survivors, very different from the apple-cheeked activists of leftist poster art. The martyred girl Zhang Zhixin, killed in 1975 for speaking out against the Gang of Four, became a favorite theme. Amateur and "unofficial" artists organized themselves, one Beijing group, the "star" group, even demonstrating in the streets for the right to exhibit its modernistic works.[5]

Films dealt with such hitherto taboo subjects as political divorces caused by the Anti-rightist Movement, the violence of Red Guard factional struggles, and the suffering of intellectuals who were persecuted to death during the Cultural Revolution. In dance, abstract themes and modern-dance movements appeared, along with the large-scale revival of the ethnic minority and Han (ethnic Chinese) folk dances that had been suppressed as backward and divisive during the Cultural Revolution. Among literature and art theorists, debates on whether literature and art could entertain as well as instruct, on whether an artistic product had to be understood by *all* the masses, and on whether self-expression had a role in creativity became possible for the first time. Liter-

ature and the arts were generally just as political as they had
been during the Cultural Revolution, but at last they were
beginning to convey messages the people wanted to hear—
indeed, needed desperately to hear as they tried to come to
terms with the trauma they had been through and with the
imperfect world that so little resembled the socialist paradise
they had been promised.

The Chinese Communist party's involvement with literature and the arts dates from well before the revolution, with
the formation of the League of Left-Wing Writers in 1930
in Shanghai. Since Chairman Mao's "Talks at the Yanan
Forum on Literature and Art" in 1942, the party has explicitly asserted that literature and art should serve political pur-
poses, and that in evaluating individual works, political criteria should take precedence over aesthetic ones. Criticisms
of works of literature and art have often signaled the begin-
nings of political movements, just as they signaled the beginning of a party rectification in Yanan in 1942. The Anti-
rightist Movement of 1957 attacked many of the writers and
artists who had spoken out during the "Hundred Flowers"
liberalization of the year before; the Cultural Revolution
began with the criticism of a historical drama, "Hai Rui
Dismissed from Office," in 1965. The upheaval was called a
"cultural" revolution because Mao saw how an attack on
"bourgeois" writers, artists, and academics could help him
regain power within the party; that such a revolution
should be capable of creating a near civil war and bringing
the economy close to a standstill is an indication of the
political sensitivity of the arts in China. The "eight model
theatrical works" that replaced other performances, and the
sterile "revolutionary" stories and poster arts of that era,
became open political propaganda—weapons for exposing
the "treason" of Mao's enemies.

After the fall of the Gang of Four in 1976, the party softened the description of its relationship to literature and art
from "leading" to "guiding." On July 26, 1980, the slogan
"Literature in the service of the people and in the service of
socialism" replaced that of "Literature in the service of politics."[6] Even so, post–Cultural Revolution artistic production has been primarily dictated by political considerations.
The arts have still been seen as tools for educating people
in correct values and attitudes; artists and writers are still
called "engineers of the human soul," "workers on the
thought education front," and "propagandists of the party
line." As Perry Link points out in his superb introduction
to the anthology *Stubborn Weeds*, out of the five elements
involved in literary production, readers, writers, editors and
publishers, critics, and party leaders, the primary relationship in China has been that between readers and party leaders, while the other three participants have been seen as
intermediaries, as tools for transmitting certain attitudes
and policies. Even if the party no longer insists that all
works must be understood by the lowest common denom-
inator (workers, peasants, and soldiers), in practice the
"message" must still be very obvious or it runs the risk of
being criticized for "abstraction" or "obscurity," and of
being withheld or withdrawn. It must, in addition, harmo-
nize with the current "spirit" of the party's policies. Relative
"looseness," or liberalization, occurs when it suits the needs
of a controlling faction in its struggles against another faction; "tightness," or restriction, quickly ensues when writers
and artists go too far.

Even before China became a socialist country, Chinese
writers and artists had a long tradition of social concern.
From China's famous poet Qu Yuan, who is said to have
drowned himself in 278 B.C. in protest against his weak government, to Du Fu (A.D. 712–770), who spoke out for the

poor and hungry, to the late Qing dynasty novelists and the twentieth-century May Fourth Movement political activists, China's writers have frequently seen their work as a conduit for speaking for the people and helping the leadership carry out its responsibility to them. Painters, too, have made social comments through the use of symbolism, particularly during rule by foreign dynasties. To a great extent, then, China's *engagé* tradition in the arts made Leninist-style control of them relatively easy: in the exciting early period of the party's ambitions, the values of the party closely matched those of many of China's writers and artists; to speak for socialism was often tantamount to speaking out against society's injustices. This was especially true during the 1950s, when revolutionary idealism among China's intellectuals ran high.

Yet there has also been a parallel strain of "art of art's sake" among China's artists, connected with the traditional Daoist emphasis on withdrawal from the social world, and with artists' involvement with nature and appreciation of decorative beauty. This heritage, combined with contemporary writers' and artists' sense of responsibility to denounce and try to correct the social inequities that have emerged under Maoist socialism, has created considerable chafing against policies that limit literature and the arts. The Cultural Revolution taught many that self-sacrifice was useless and dangerous, and led to a rediscovery of the value of the individual and a desire, particularly among younger writers and artists, for "self-expression." This has often been anathema to a party that requires subservience to the state.

The experiences of many writers and artists during the Cultural Revolution were so dreadful that they gained a new kind of courage. They saw close colleagues persecuted and killed, and they felt the guilt of survivors. Many are convinced that they have already seen the worst, and that little can frighten them now. After the death of Mao, many proved willing to take the risk, even in the face of criticism, of portraying injustices truthfully (Liu Binyan and Bai Hua are the two writers most noted for their outspokenness, but there are many others). Although the controls are still many and the obstacles to artistic freedom great, penalties for unorthodoxy are nowhere near as extreme as they once were.

During those comparatively golden years, from the end of 1978, when the Third Plenary Session of the 11th Party Committee called for "liberation of thought," to the early months of 1981, when the criticism of Bai Hua's filmscript *Unrequited Love* signaled the end of the period of greatest freedom until that time, China's writers and artists drew on the great unhappiness of the Cultural Revolution and the thoughtfulness the tragedy taught them. What the Mao period covered over with leftist prettinesses and revolutionary heroes, they now exposed with emotion, satire, and bitterness. Particularly in literature, the range of subjects was broad and many forbidden areas were broached for the first time. Readers encountered worlds they themselves knew· worlds of economic backwardness and disorder, impoverished countrysides, and tense human relationships. There were factories incapacitated by heavy bureaucratic systems and corruption, privileged officials abusing their positions to oppress the people, young people driven to commit crimes, their idealism trampled on by a hypocritical revolution.

The exciting and popular writers of the period were not so much the older ones like Ding Ling, who had been persecuted for so long that she seemed sustained only by her stubborn faith in the party, but the middle-aged and new young writers. Some of the most courageous middle-aged writers, like Liu Binyan and Bai Hua, had been labeled rightists in 1957. Their reputations were now restored. The younger writers, a great many of them women, had been buffeted by the Cultural Revolution, lived in the countryside for years as "educated youths," and had thought deeply about the promises of socialism and their betrayed ideals. When they had the chance to create, they did not repeat slogans and clichés in praise of the system that had brought them so little happiness; instead, they portrayed what they saw as the truth. Often, they probed the deeper reasons why China had come to be what it was.

Few, if any, of the works produced during those years may be considered great or even particularly good by world standards. They suffer from an obviousness, a heavy moralistic hand, and a lack of technical sophistication. Still, many are powerful for their expression of themes and questions important to the Chinese people. Some of the bold expressions in the "wound" literature, in the "thoughtful" (*fansi*) literature, in the literature about post–Cultural Revolution reforms, in the exposé literature, in the love stories and other humanistic stories, and in the literature which experimented with new techniques would later become targets of criticism. But in the meantime, there was a time of taboo-breaking courage.

The earliest literary breakthrough came with the publication of "Homeroom Teacher" (*Ban Zhuren*) by Liu Xinwu in November 1977.[7] The story raises questions about juvenile delinquency, but more important, it shows how politics has ruined a "good" child, another character who has become an obedient political machine through her "revolutionary education." The genre to which it belongs is named after another early work, a story called "Wound" (*Shangheng*) by Lu Xinhua[8] that tells of a young woman's tense relations with her mother and with her boyfriend because of political pressures. In the flood of stories written in imitation, "wound literature" came to mean all the works that reflected the pain and injustice of the Cultural Revolution.

"Thoughtful" literature began to emerge in 1979, so called because it touches on the causes of the unhappiness rather than simply describing it. It explores such sensitive questions as the responsibility of Chairman Mao and the nature of socialism. The most famous example is the story by Gao Xiaosheng "Chen Huansheng Comes to Town" (*Chen Huansheng Jin Cheng*).[9] A peasant goes to market to earn money to buy a hat, but becomes ill and has to stay at the county reception station. A seemingly generous party leader arranges this and even takes him there in his private car. However, the cost of the lodging is so great that the peasant must use up the money he had planned to spend on a hat. He consoles himself by reflecting that only he, of all his acquaintances, has had the opportunity to ride in a car and stay overnight in such a grand place.

The story, which Chinese find most amusing, raises questions about whether the apparent concern of the party leader for an ordinary person in fact brings him happiness. It is also about the self-deception of the people, who persuade themselves they are content when they are actually being oppressed, a familiar, ironic theme in modern Chinese literature best exemplified by the mental antics of Lu Xun's famous self-deceiver, Ah Q. Another subject of the story is the gap between the countryside and the city, between the privileged life styles of high leaders and the impoverished lives of the peasants.

The reformers and the enormous difficulties they faced became a third common literary theme—the voice of the Deng faction in fiction. Jiang Zilong's "Manager Qiao Assumes Office" (*Qiao Changzhang Shang Renji*),[10] for example, describes a chaotic and mismanaged factory that symbolizes China itself. Although Qiao finally meets certain production quotas, he encounters great resistance along the way, and the writer's implication is that the tasks before the reformers are so great that without support they may not succeed. Zhang Jie's novel *Heavy Wings (Chenzhong de Chibang)*,[11] is also set largely in a factory. Here even the reformers, doing their best to realize the Four Modernizations, are burdened by traditional feudal ideas, and they lead a corps of officials who have alienated the people.

Love, enjoying a huge comeback after the Cultural Revolution, was one of the most popular of literary subjects in these years, but it was to become one of the most criticized because such stories often asserted the primacy of human feelings over political considerations. Yu Mei's "Ah, People" *(A, Ren)*[12] is about the love between a girl sold into a landlord's family as a concubine and the landlord's son. After Liberation, they are not permitted to be together because the son is from a bad class background. Only after the fall of the Gang of Four, when the son's landlord "cap," or label, is removed, are they able at last to marry.

Jin Fang's *Open Love Letter (Gongkai de Qingshu)*,[13] a novella, describes the triangular love between a woman and two men, one of whom she finally rejects. In traditional Chinese terms, a person is expected to have only one love in a lifetime, so such a breakup seemed unorthodox, even immoral. Yet young people welcomed Jin's description of someone who places the fulfillment of individual happiness above traditional morality, and the story was extremely popular.

"Love Cannot Be Forgotten" *(Ai, Shi Bu Neng Wangjide)* by Zhang Jie also raises the question of the oppressive weight of tradition. It tells how a divorced woman writer falls in love with a party official whose marriage is based on revolutionary duty (the woman's father saved his life). The divorcée sacrifices the relationship for the sake of her beloved's wife, telling herself that she may be united with him in the hereafter. The story was one of the first to treat the subject of loveless marriages, of which there are many in China. It was considered unusual also for its portrayal of a party leader as a flesh-and-blood human being rather than as a mechanistically perfect ideologue.

Many other stories of the period emphasized the value of the individual, and were among those most fiercely attacked when the winds shifted again. Li Ping's *When Sunset Disappears* (*Wanxia Xiaoshi de Shihou*)[14] depicts the relationship between the descendants of a Guomindang (KMT) general and a Communist one, implying (as does "Ah, People") that class background and politics may not be of primary importance after all. Another important humanistic work, Dai Houying's *People, Ah People* (*Ren, A Ren*),[15] tells how a group of college students who graduated during the 1950s lives through the Anti-rightist Movement and the Cultural Revolution, and of their disillusionment with socialism. Shen Rong's screenplay *When People Reach Middle Age*[16] (*Ren Dao Zhongnian*), later made into an award-winning film which was withdrawn during the 1983 campaign against spiritual pollution, concerns the plight of intellectuals: it contrasts the professional dedication of a female doctor with the self-righteous power of the wife of an official, who spouts revolutionary slogans and emphasizes ideology and rank.

"Reportage" or "exposé" literature, best exemplified by the work of Liu Binyan, and particularly by his long report "Between Men and Demons," focuses on corruption and abuses of privilege. "Between Men and Demons" is the true story of a northwestern county that Liu visited, and it tells about the vast power of the local party secretary and how she came to wield it. The play *If I Were Real* also deals with corruption and the manipulation of connections. This time, however, the protagonist pretends to be a high official's son and deceives party leaders at their own connection game.

Another important exposé, Wang Jing's screenplay *In the Files of Society (Zai Shehui de Dangan Li)*,[17] recounts the rape of a young girl by a high official and his son. After the girl marries, her husband, discovering that she is not a virgin, drives her out. She becomes a hoodlum and an outcast and is eventually arrested. During her trial, she is unable to bring the official and his son to justice because they are too powerful. They drive off in their private car and she goes to prison. The title implies that such cases cannot achieve fair treatment in official files—it is only in the hearts of ordinary people that right is distinguished from wrong.

Corruption was also treated in poetry, as in the noted "General, You Shouldn't Do That." Ye Wenfu exposes a military official who hasn't learned anything from being persecuted during the Cultural Revolution: he tears down a kindergarten to build himself an expensive home. It is said that the general is supposed to be Wang Dongxing, Mao's personal bodyguard and a notorious "whateverist"—so this exposé had its obvious uses for the reformers. Experimental poet Shu Ting deals with the loyalty of a lover to a Cultural Revolution victim in her poem "?":[18]

> Now let them shoot at me
> I shall walk calmly across the land
> Towards you, towards you
> My long hair blowing in the wind
> I am your wild lily of the storm

Unique to poetry was the strong current of abstraction, which seemed strange and unfamiliar to Chinese so accustomed to the blatantly obvious literature of revolution. Such experiments would later earn the works of many young poets the critical label "obscure poetry" (*menglong shi*) and their subsequent denunciation by the older generation. One such, Gu Cheng's "One Generation" (*Yidai Ren*),[19] here printed in its entirety, was considered too difficult for readers to understand:

> The black night has given me black eyes,
> Yet I use them to search for light.

The poem evidently refers to the scars of the Cultural Revolution and the tragedy's gift to its victims of an ability to seek a greater understanding. Gu again sounds the theme of optimism born of despair in his "Feeling" (*Ganjue*):[20]

> The sky is gray
> The road is gray
> The building is gray
> The rain is gray

> In this blanket of dead gray
> Two children walk by,
> One bright red
> One pale green.

These stories and poems may seem tame enough by Western standards, but Chinese fans considered them extremely daring, and as each taboo was broken, a sense of exhilaration followed. It seemed that literature and the arts were no longer to be tools for waging class struggle. They had to praise socialism, of course, but they could also expose injustice; they could be written not only for workers, peasants, and soldiers, but also for intellectuals. They could describe real situations and real people, real feelings and real dilemmas. They could probe the past, and express aspirations for a less political future.

These notions were not clearly established victories, however. Rather, they were the subjects of ongoing debates, and those people advocating greater restrictions waged counter-attacks. Indeed, the seeds for later controls were planted early on, some as early as the spring of 1979. After the arrest of the democratic activist Wei Jingsheng, and Deng Xiaoping's mention of the "Four Basic Principles" (establishing socialism, Marxism–Leninism–Mao Zedong Thought, the party, and "the people's democratic dictatorship" as unvarying facts of Chinese life), the literary and art worlds were quick to follow the cooling trend. In April 1979 Guangdong Province's *Southern Daily (Nanfang Ribao)* and *Guangdong Daily (Guangdong Ribao)* published a series of articles calling for a "forward-looking" literature—works describing the dark side of life were said to be retrogressive. The May 18, 1979, *People's Daily* printed an article that was a bad portent for "thoughtful" literature: a Shanghai middle-school student had written a composition describing how he saw a woman and child begging in front of the "Great Brightness Movie Theater" and suddenly felt that the brightness was not so bright after all. His teacher, who was praised for "grasping political thought work," insisted that he rewrite the paper, and sent him for coaching sessions with a political cadre. Then in June 1979 *Hebei Literature and Art (Hebei Wenyi)* published an article called "Praise and Shame" (*Gede yu Quede*) by someone no one had heard of named Li Jian. Li claimed that it was shameful not to praise socialism and Chairman Mao, and that the hidden motive of some of those exposing the Gang of Four was to oppose the party and socialism.

It was widely recognized that Li was speaking on behalf of certain high party officials, as is often the case when a prominent article by a complete unknown is published. But a response backed by reformers in the party soon followed. In the July 20 *Guangming Daily*, the veteran theorist Wang Ruowang spoke in defense of intellectuals against the "praise faction." Others rallied around, and Li Jian became an outcast. It is even said that his girlfriend left him and that he tried to kill himself. However, Deng Xiaoping himself is said to have asked writers to help Li learn from his mistakes, and he later published again in a different spirit.[21]

The Fourth Congress of Writers and Artists held in the autumn of 1979 simultaneously echoed the intense convictions of many writers and artists that more freedom was necessary and sounded a warning note that greater control was in the winds. This conference, the only one of its importance held in post–Cultural Revolution China until the Writers' Conference of 1984–1985, bore the seeds of the tensions that were to become even more acute in 1983.[22]

Deng Xiaoping's "Congratulatory Message"[23] to the congress conveyed conflicting signals. On the one hand, he spoke for literary and artistic freedom:

The unhampered development of different styles in creative works and free discussion of thought in literary and art theories should all be encouraged . . . writers and artists should prevent and overcome the tendency of monotonous formulism and jargonism.

In mental endeavors as complicated as literature and art, it is absolutely essential for writers and artists to totally utilize their individual creative spirit. Writers and artists must have the freedom to choose their subject matter and method of presentation based upon artistic practice and exploration. No interference in this regard can be permitted.

However, in the same speech, Deng outlined a specific content for literature and the arts that left very little room for choice:

The sole criterion for deciding the correctness of all work should be whether that work is helpful or harmful to the accomplishment of the Four Modernizations.

and later:

Writers and artists should portray pioneers in the Four Modernizations drive. They should vividly depict the pioneers' revolutionary ideals and scientific approaches, their noble sentiments and
creations, their great vision, and their down-to-earth attitude.
Writers and artists should use the pioneers' new images to whip
up enthusiasm for socialism among our masses.

In a very different spirit were the speeches of a number of
writers. Bai Hua's speech, "No Breakthrough, No Literature,"[24] told movingly of the sacrifices made during the Cultural Revolution and called for artistic freedom. On literary
subject matter, he said:

Should we cover up social contradictions that no one can possibly
cover up? Should we sing the praises of the ignorance that caused
our people to suffer great losses? Should we keep silent about the
bureaucratism that even now impedes our forward motion?

On speech:

I often hear comrades with children say apprehensively, "My son
is bound to go to prison someday, because he doesn't know how
to lie." And some comrades say with smug satisfaction, "My son
is bound to make something of himself, because at his age he is
already a double-dealer."

and:

Just what sort of socialist nation is this where Communist party
members don't dare speak the truth at party meetings; where
fathers and sons, brothers, sisters, and friends cannot confide in
one another; where writers dare not jot down thoughts in note-
books and citizens dare not keep diaries?

On associations:

Beginning in 1957, when "secretive personal associations" became
grounds for criminal charges, who dared to keep up his personal
associations? . . . It has gotten somewhat better the last three
years, but comrades whose fears have not yet abated still dare not
go to gatherings of intellectuals. As soon as a large number get

together, they get nervous. For a number of years, we weren't able to let each other know who was dead and who was alive.

The elderly dramatist Xia Yan said in his speech:

I have written only one play since Liberation. This was the worst piece I ever created because I worried over each sentence, wondering whether or not it would conflict with party policy.

However, he sounded a moderating note, urging writers to exercise restraint in exposing the injustices of the Cultural Revolution:

I was imprisoned for eight years and forced to write nearly a thousand confessions. I need not mention the beatings and personal insults I suffered. A foreign friend suggested that I describe these experiences. As a Communist party member and a patriot, I felt that I should not. To reveal that fascism is still strong in China could frighten the people. We must not follow in the steps of a certain writer from the Soviet Union who specialized in writing about political prison camps and went to Western countries to publish his works. This course of action does not benefit the Chinese people, nor does it strengthen our unity and stability.[25]

In his final address, moreover, Xia offered thoughts that were in accord with what was soon to become the dominant spirit for literature and the arts:

I believe that before setting pen to paper, a patriotic writer, a progressive writer, and especially a writer who is a member of the Communist party, will certainly consider how to so render the themes, events, and characters in which he is interested so as to make them contribute toward rousing the revolutionary spirit and raising moral and aesthetic levels; he must be aware of the heavy burden of responsibility he bears for the motherland and the people.[26]

In Xia Yan's words, a growing gap between younger and older intellectuals emerges. While the older ones have suffered, if anything, even more than the younger, they are less willing to speak out, convinced that to do so is in some way to betray the party, to create differences and tensions, and to fail to fulfill a patriotic responsibility. For younger intellectuals, who are also motivated by patriotism, speaking out is the way to play a constructive role. In future campaigns, the party would use the more restrained older intellectuals to contain the younger ones, and their important mediating role would prove more effective than coarser methods. The other gap reflected in the Fourth Congress was, of course, that between the party and writers and artists in general, even the most conservative of whom chafed under restrictions on their freedom to create as they wished.

Thus although many of the speeches at the congress called boldly for democracy and artistic independence, some given by party leaders and older intellectuals contained a hidden trap. The "spring of literature and art" was said to have returned, but even at its greenest there were hints of a winter to come.

A Darker Time

Almost immediately after the Fourth Congress closed in the fall of 1979, the trial and harsh sentencing of Wei Jingsheng sent a cold wind across China.

Wei was the editor of the unofficial magazine *Explorations* (*Tansuo*), and his earlier arrest in March of that year, together with some of the other "counterrevolutionaries" in his circle, had sounded a clear warning. However, the debates at the Democracy Walls and "doubts about socialism" continued. Some unofficial magazines, such as the famous *Today* (*Jintian*), sought to compromise with the party by being purely literary. Others sought the protection of sympathetic high party leaders. Still others decided to moderate their views. Then in November Wei was convicted of giving state secrets to foreigners and of inciting people to overturn the dictatorship of the proletariat. He got fifteen years.

In a January 16, 1980, speech published in *People's Daily*, Deng Xiaoping announced the Central Committee's decision to rescind the "Four Great" guarantees of free expression, including the rights to "speak out freely, air views fully, put up big character posters, and hold great debates."[1] The justification was that, given the constitutional guarantees of freedom of belief, speech, press, assembly, association, procession, and demonstration, such expressions were unnecessary leftovers from Cultural Revolution–style politics. The right to strike was revoked as well, ostensibly because, under socialism, there was no "contradiction" between workers and leaders. The example of Poland must have been quite worrisome.

Deng's speech also criticized young people for infatuation with "bourgeois liberalism." It might be correct to say that literature did not have to "serve" politics, he said, but it was incorrect to think that it could be separated from politics. Soon after, General Party Secretary Hu Yaobang gave the keynote address at a Conference on Playwriting held in Beijing from January 23 to February 13. Although his tone was conciliatory, promising noninterference with the arts and official sanction for exposé literature as long as it contributed to the Four Modernizations, he specifically criticized three works, a play and two screenplays: Sha Yexin's *If I Were Real* for making a hero of a swindler; Wang Jing's film script *In the Files of Society* (about the girl raped by the party leader and his son), for exaggeration; and another script, *Girl Thief (Nü Zei),*[2] by Li Kewei, for creating sympathy with a young hoodlum who outwits the police. All three of these works were said to describe young protagonists on the wrong side of the law, "negative" models rather than the socialist heroes readers were supposed to emulate.

In March 1980 the slogan "Writers should consider the social effects of their writing" was widely promulgated; according to the critics, certain children had murdered their brothers and sisters after seeing a violent imported movie.[3] However, on July 26 the slogan "Literature in the service of the people and in the service of socialism" was announced, modifying the old "Literature in the service of politics." Perhaps encouraged by this, literary experimentation continued, and on October 10 the veteran film star Zhao Dan, knowing he was about to die of cancer, delivered his famous plea for artistic freedom, published in the *People's Daily*: "If the party controls literature and art too tightly, there is no hope for them, they are finished."

The elections held in the autumn of 1980 for representatives to local-level People's Congresses went well beyond acceptable bounds in some university districts. At the Hunan Teachers' College, Beijing University, Fudan University, and Guizhou University, among others, the students took the elections as opportunities to express their views and test the "democracy" the elections were said to represent. Some candidates nominated themselves, gave campaign speeches, and developed political platforms. Some were non-Marxists and others openly critical of their local party leaders. They spoke on concrete matters such as arbitrary job assignments, crowded living conditions, and unsanitary and unnutritious dining-hall food, and on abstract questions such as democracy and freedom of speech. Some even called for the election of all officials right up to premier. When the leaders in Hunan tried to make students conform to their ideas of how the elections should be conducted, there were boycotts of classes, demonstrations, and even a hunger strike.

With all this unrest at a time when the economic situation in China was less than good and plans for the development of the country were being modified as having been over-ambitious, the Deng regime put new priority on preserving party power. At the end of 1980, a "Work Meeting" of the Central Committee tolled a death knell for one of China's periods of greatest freedom. Documents approved and transmitted at that meeting signaled an alliance between reformers and conservatives within the party against anti-party forces ("Peaceful unification" was the slogan) and called for the active involvement of Communist Youth League and party members in arguing against dissenters. Another document called for the shutdown of all unofficial magazines, the arrest of those actively involved, and the investigation of those in frequent contact with them.[4]

The students and democrats had been radically mistaken about how Deng Xiaoping felt about their activities. They had believed he wanted their help in putting pressure on recalcitrant middle-level bureaucrats. Now they discovered that he was far more interested in putting pressure on them. Meetings were held that spring, criticisms and arrests were made, and the voices were silenced. Those who had participated in the election movements made obligatory recitations of loyalty to the party, socialism, and Marxism–Leninism–Mao Zedong Thought, while those involved with underground magazines were arrested and dispatched to prisons and labor camps.

The suppression of political activists was a relatively simple matter, even considering how many were willing to make things harder for themselves by refusing to recant. The control of writers and artists was a slower and more complicated business. In Leninist parlance, writers and art-

ists were "engineers of the human soul," indispensable in
helping the party instill socialist values. They could not just
be locked up and tossed away.

It is conceivable that the October Zhao Dan speech was
one of the final straws that led to the major crackdown on
"bourgeois liberalism" and on Bai Hua's *Unrequited Love* in
the spring of 1981, the main target named in the campaign.
Quite often a model selected for criticism is not the most
extreme example of the tendencies the party wishes to dis-
courage, but rather a prominent and popular example that
typifies the questions many people in the literary world and
on the streets are asking. Bai Hua's screenplay had already
been made into a film, tentatively entitled *Sun and Man*
(*Taiyang yu Ren*), the sun referring, of course, to Chairman
Mao. It describes a patriotic overseas Chinese, a painter,
who returns to China after Liberation to help build socialism. Through various political movements, especially the
Cultural Revolution, he loses his job and family, escaping
finally to a barren steppe area, where he steals food to stay
alive. At last, after walking a path which leaves a large im-
print of a question mark in the snow, he freezes to death,
the setting sun shining over his body.

For many Chinese, especially the intellectuals who had
dedicated themselves to the party and to socialism but had
been persecuted severely in return for their love, the unspoken question in the snow resonated with the many unspoken questions in their own hearts. Why, when they had
given so much of themselves, indeed, been willing to devote
their lives, had they been rewarded with such cruel treatment? Most city dwellers were personally acquainted with
those who had met their ends in similar fashion to Bai Hua's
protagonist, or had perhaps come close to doing so themselves. What the film did was bring into the open what they
had hardly dared to whisper, a questioning of the basic na-

ture of the relationship between the party and the people who had tried to do their best for it. Had they been foolish to sacrifice themselves for so little?

Since Bai Hua was an army officer, the military newspapers were the first to criticize the script *Unrequited Love* openly, for "bourgeois liberalism," on April 21, 1981. However, in an "internal" directive of March 27 limited to high officials, Deng Xiaoping had already indicated that the script had problems, bowing, perhaps, to pressure from military leaders with whom he had recently established an alliance.[5] The orthodox *Report on the Times* (*Shidai de Baogao*) soon joined in. Bai was said to have incorrectly attacked Mao and to have rejected the leadership of the party. His sentence "You love the motherland, but does the motherland love you?" was called a grave error in the representation of the relationship between the party and the people. Another unspoken problem was that Bai had made Mao's responsibility for the tragedy all too clear: the party wished to negate only certain aspects of Mao's later policies, but Bai's wholesale condemnation threatened to bring the very legitimacy of the socialist system into question.

In fact, the film had been well received by a number of high party leaders when it was submitted for inspection in early 1981. But when Deng found it objectionable it was quickly withheld from public release. The campaign attacking it lasted most of the year, but Bai Hua himself, having made the requisite self-criticism, was exempted—in fact, another screenplay of his received a prize. The message to writers and artists was clear: If you are obedient and don't overstep boundaries, you will be rewarded.

The campaign to criticize *Unrequited Love* did not work out exactly as the party had wished. Since the script was published together with the criticisms, as a negative example, the Chinese people could read the script and judge it for themselves, and they often decided they liked it very much. There were protests in defense of Bai Hua, with meetings and even big character posters (despite the ban), at some of China's major universities, particularly at Beijing University and Shanghai's Fudan University. Even less-outspoken intellectuals felt in their hearts that it was a good screenplay: the party's allegation that the situation it described was "not typical" was patently false. But resistance to the criticisms was not effective against what was apparently a decision of the Central Committee to crack down on freedom in the arts and on permissiveness in society in general.

The Sixth Plenary Session of the 11th Party Committee, which began on June 29, 1981, was important for making some of the boundaries on intellectual and artistic freedom official. In addition to establishing the triumvirate of Deng Xiaoping, Hu Yaobang, and Zhao Ziyang as China's most powerful leaders, its main task was the evaluation of Chairman Mao's role in history. The outcome, a disappointment to those who believed Mao as much responsible as the Gang of Four for bringing China near civil war and economic collapse, was the official position that he had made great contributions in the earlier part of his career, but had begun to "make mistakes" with the Anti-rightist Movement in 1957. The errors of Mao the man were not considered to have detracted from the greatness of Mao Zedong Thought, which was still to be the central guiding spirit of the Chinese Communist party.

During the same meeting, the "Four Basic Principles" (also known as the "Four Upholds") were officially established as the guiding slogan for the new period. They are: Uphold Marxism–Leninism–Mao Zedong Thought; Uphold the leadership of the Communist party; Uphold the people's democratic dictatorship; Uphold the socialist road.

The Four Basic Principles provided ammunition against those expressing dissatisfaction with the status quo. They became the standards against which to measure thought, speech, and behavior, as well as any artistic product, be it literature, art, drama, film, or dance. Beliefs, views, or activities seen as conflicting with the Principles could be criticized and outlawed; if the "meaning" of a literary or art work didn't uphold the Principles, the work could be withheld or withdrawn. From the spring of 1981 when Deng first mentioned the slogan, through the campaign against bourgeois liberalism of that summer and fall, all the way through the "warming" of the early months of 1983 and its climax in March with the outspoken speeches on the 100th anniversary of the death of Karl Marx, the Four Basic Principles were often-mentioned themes of Chinese political life, defining the limits beyond which it was not permitted to go. In a typical Chinese Catch-22, they determined whether or not people were considered fit to enjoy freedoms of belief, speech, art, and information; only if people upheld the Four Basic Principles were they entitled to the freedoms outlined in the Chinese constitution.

On July 17, 1981, Deng Xiaoping made a speech to Propaganda Ministry leaders (made public in the August 21 *People's Daily*), cautioning that "What we have to pay more attention to is the existing lax, weak, soft, scattered situation. . . . In our work on the ideological front there still exist leftist tendencies and this must be changed, but this is not to say we should not hold criticism/self-criticism about the liberal tendencies."[6]

The newspapers took up the movement to criticize bourgeois liberalism, and General Party Secretary Hu Yaobang, in an August 31 meeting on ideological questions, emphasized the importance of criticizing *Unrequited Love*.[7] In another speech at the celebrations of the 100th anniversary of the birth of the writer Lu Xun in September of that year, he talked about the "critical need to maintain vigilance," although the troublemakers were said to be only a tiny minority, "like lice on the body of a lion."[8]

Despite the chilly wind of the spring, summer, and early fall of 1981, the movement against bourgeois liberalism never succeeded in controlling writers and artists fully. First of all, the party's mistakes were perceived as being much greater than those described in *Unrequited Love*, so silent support for the screenplay was widespread. Second, the Central Committee leaders' direct involvement with the movement did not sit well with people: Bai Hua's self-criticism had clearly been induced and he had had no opportunity to defend himself. Therefore, the party tried a different tactic, as presaged at the Fourth Congress when, in the move against "obscure poetry," it had used older poets as ammunition against younger ones.

One of the first criticisms of obscure poetry (which by the autumn of 1981 had become quite a literary school, with theory to back it), may be found in the October 1980 issue of *Poetry*, in an article by the experimental poet Gu Cheng's own father, the old poet Gu Gong. Called "Two Generations," the article does not condemn the new poetry outright, but complains that it is impossible to understand, for there is too great a gap between the old and the young poets' generations. Then in 1981, party literary officials began to complain that the "obscurity" (*menglong* may also be translated as "vagueness") of the poetry was not merely a literary question. It reflected confusion in the minds of the young poets and their generation, and it was hence a social problem. Readers' difficulty in understanding such work, the officials claimed, proved that it lacked the quality of inspiring them to contribute to the Four Modernizations and socialism.

With the party's encouragement, some of the older poets such as Ai Qing, Zhang Kejia, and Tian Jian began to write articles criticizing the new poetry. In an April 1981 issue of Shanghai's *Literary Report* (*Wenxue Bao*), Zhang Kejia published his "About Obscure Poetry," calling it a poisonous, hateful phenomenon. The climax of the criticism movement came in November with a flood of meetings and articles, published primarily in *Literature and Art Bulletin*. The result was to stem the outpouring of new poetry. The older poets had muted the younger ones, where more direct participation from the Central Committee in the case of Bai Hua had failed.

The third target of major attack was love stories. This campaign also reached its climax in November 1981. In the November 4 *People's Daily*, an article called "Earnestly Discuss the Expression of Love in Literature and Art" drew attention to the portrayal of love in the arts, and articles in *Literature and Art Bulletin* soon followed. The articles said that from the time of the Fourth Congress, film, television, art, music, drama, and literature had begun to show an "unhealthy tendency" in the description of love. This was not a question of creative method but one of correct political standpoint. There was an overemphasis on love, as if some writers and artists felt that without love there could be no art. Writers were discussing complicated love relationships, even relationships between Chinese and foreigners, thus setting up a contradiction between love and socialist morality. Now writers and artists were requested not to put love in an "unsuitable position" in first place of importance.

Soon, most provincial newspapers, magazines, and arts associations were involved in the criticism of the artistic

treatment of love, and General Party Secretary Hu Yaobang
made a December 27 speech to representatives of the National Feature Film Creator's meeting emphasizing the party's concern about the question:

Our art and literary works must first teach people to love the
mother country's socialist cause, and if necessary, to sacrifice their
own lives and loves. If you say that everything is for love, that
love is important above all, this is not correct.[9]

Among the works named for criticism, Jin Fang's *Open Love
Letter* received much of the brunt, for lacking socialist
morality and looking too favorably on the individual pur-
suit of happiness. Yu Mei's "Ah, People" was said to be
propagandizing the commonality of human feelings above
class loyalties, and a Guizhou journal, *Flower and Stream*
(*Huaxi*), published a self-criticism for having made an error
of judgment in publishing the story. Dai Houying's *People,
Ah, People* was discussed in Guangzhou's *Southern Daily* for
entire months, with special columns, from the end of 1981
to April 1982. On April 29 a judgment was finally announced: the novel was said to "use bourgeois humanist
thought to view life." The works earlier criticized in the 1980
dramatists' meeting, *If I Were Real, In the Files of Society*, and
Girl Thief, were also given another round of criticism, often
in the *China Youth Daily* (*Zhongguo Qingnian Bao*), accused
again of exacerbating social conflicts and making hoodlums
into heroes for young people to identify with.

For some time following these campaigns, outspoken literary experiments became muted. Wound literature disappeared. Writers and artists obediently described the bright,
not the dark, side of life. They created socialist heroes con-
tributing to the Four Modernizations. Once again, workers,
peasants, and soldiers appeared as the main characters—
there had been too many intellectuals—and as for love, it

was neither too tragic nor too sweet, lest individual interests sap revolutionary ardor. By the 12th National Congress of the Chinese Communist party in September 1982, most writers and artists were busy propagandizing the brightness of socialism and the victories of the party. Still, the economic experiments with decentralization were reaffirmed by that congress, and the new social freedoms that were corollaries of the reforms continued to develop. Controls of literature and the arts remained less effective than in the past.

II

A Shifting Season: 1983

An Erratic Climate

If the early 1980s saw swings in the climate for intellectual freedom, 1983 saw the greatest swings of all. The crisis of confidence in the party and in socialism continued to be a problem among young people who felt their "crisis" was justified and craved greater freedom of expression. It posed a challenge to the power holders, who felt pressure to combat the crisis by restoring party integrity and by proving that Chinese socialism could be an economic success. Despite attempts by the Deng regime to improve moral standards among party leaders and to encourage old leaders to retire to advisory positions, widespread corruption and incompetence continued. The government's inability to keep pace with rapidly rising consumer expectations was another source of discontent, exacerbated by greater contact with a wealthier outside world. Meanwhile, young people's "disorderly imitation" (*luanxue*) of the West contributed to what party leaders and members of the older generation often saw as a breakdown of morality and social order. Contradictory party policies made it difficult to resolve these tensions, as the party sought to improve China's economic situation with still more liberal reforms, while trying to retain the obedience of the people by exerting greater social and ideological control.

During the post–Cultural Revolution period, China's doors had gradually, if not always steadily, opened wider, admitting hundreds of thousands of tourists, business people, foreign teachers and students, and technical advisers. There were 5,300 foreign students in China in 1983, while since 1978 China had sent abroad 18,500 officially sponsored students, and an additional 7,000 had found their way out on their own. By 1983 there were more than 10,000 Chinese students studying in the U.S. alone, and delegations were visiting in record numbers.[1] Special Economic Zones had been set up in Guangdong and Fujian Provinces to operate along administrative and economic lines more conducive to doing business with capitalist countries. Regulations had been liberalized by 1983 to permit some local companies to sign contracts with foreign businesses without approval from the central level. They had also been revised to encourage even more foreign investment. Taxes on foreign firms were reduced, double taxation was prevented, and restrictions on the sale of goods within China were being lifted.

All this meant considerable foreign influence, and not necessarily the kind the party wanted. The party revived Mao's old slogan "Use foreign things to serve China" (*yang wei zhong yong*), advocating the importation of foreign science and technology but not foreign "thought." But the Chinese people, especially the disillusioned young, were eager for new ideas, and the materialistic trend that was sweeping the country by 1983 made curiosity about Western goods and living standards the norm. People were often more concerned about how to save money for a tape recorder, television, or even, in the big cities, a refrigerator or washing machine, than almost anything else. They now commonly saw foreign tourists, in their colorful Western clothing, pull out what seemed like a lifetime's savings in shops. They envied them the luxury hotels (by Chinese standards) that they themselves could not enter, and their comfortable travel in imported air-conditioned buses. They stared at their watches and camera equipment, and coveted their freedom to come and go. The many Chinese who had relatives abroad, especially in the southeast coastal region where most overseas Chinese emigrate from, looked to their relatives to upgrade their living standards and began to dream of going abroad themselves. In university language departments, foreign teachers brought in books and knowledge of the outside world. The publishing houses began to print translations of foreign literature in tremendous quantity, with its inevitable complement of individualism, excitement, and eroticism. Chinese television, too, from around 1980 had begun to use U.S. and British satellite news; for the first time, Chinese people could see what the rest of the world looked like on a regular basis.

By 1983 this had contributed to greater discontent with low salaries and controlled living conditions. An unprecedented number of young people had become involved in crimes, many of them thefts or illegal schemes to get rich quick, to satisfy their dreams. A derisive indifference to ideology, propaganda, and politics had become the norm even among law-abiding youths. A form of black humor was common among young Chinese—the repetition of any of the slogans in ordinary conversation was almost certain to bring a laugh. Premarital sex increased in the cities, prostitution returned, and even imported pornographic videotapes were shown rather widely. Overseas, there were more defections than ever before, including that of the tennis player Hu Na in early 1983 and those of a number of pilots who flew to Taiwan (one of them, embarrassingly for the regime, the grandson of China's most touted modern writer, Lu Xun). As of 1983 more than a thousand requests from Chinese for political asylum were pending in the U.S. alone.[2] A jetliner was hijacked to South Korea in May of that year, and several other hijacking attempts were made. In Canada, the first Chinese to receive a Ph.D. abroad since the Cultural Revolution announced that he would stay in the West to found the dissident "China Spring" movement.

In an attempt, then, to control the young more effectively, 1983 saw increased "political thought work." On January 3 it was announced that foreign records, tapes, and videotapes could no longer be imported from abroad.[3] (This was, of course, impossible to enforce.) The movement to build a "socialist spiritual civilization" through the Five Stresses (civilization, courtesy, sanitation, order, and ethics), Four Beauties (of mind, language, conduct, and environment), and Three Ardent Loves (of the motherland, socialism, and the party) reached a new height on February 24 with the television appearance of Premier Zhao Ziyang announcing the formation of a "National Five Stresses, Four Beauties, Three Ardent Loves Committee." In the spring, renewed attention was placed on combatting "smuggling" (which often meant the illegal buying and selling of imported goods such as Hong Kong sunglasses, or of domestic antiques for the foreign market) and other economic crimes.

The movement for greater internal control became most intense during the campaign to "eradicate spiritual pollution" of mid-October to mid-December 1983, one of the repressive but short-lived political movements of the post-Mao period. The movement, initially launched against "polluting" ideas in ideology, literature, and art (said to be responsible for "shaking the confidence" of China's young people), soon spread to many sectors of the country, expanding well beyond the scope originally intended. A significant portion of officials, dissatisfied with the economic reforms and with the openness to the West, seized upon the movement as an excuse to oppose everything from the contract system between peasant families and the state for what amounted to private land, to permanent waves and high heels; they also saw their chance to consolidate their power before a party rectification, or purge, scheduled for 1984, would bring them under scrutiny.

Chinese Communist Party Document No. 1 issued in January 1983, "On Consolidating and Stabilizing the Production Responsibility System in the Countryside," was a signal for many sectors of the economy to apply or extend the economic reforms. For peasants, the "responsibility system," which had its seeds in Anhui Province in 1978, meant that a family could contract for a piece of land and, after fulfilling a government quota, could grow what they wished and dispose of the harvest as they pleased, often selling it in the reopened farmers' markets. This provided an incentive to work hard, and production had risen astronomically. Chinese peasants were no longer the most disadvantaged social group. The peasants who had carried out the new system had been worried, however, about how long it would last: peasants in those areas which had not yet applied it had hesitated for the same reason. Document No. 1 brought reassurance, and spurred production even further.

In the cities, the reforms meant not only that factories were responsible for their own profits and losses, but that individual workers or groups of workers could compete with each other to contract with their management to complete a block of work for a fixed price. It was thus in their interest to work efficiently and well. Beginning in early 1983, this contract system was widely applied even in the performing arts. Performers were permitted to form their own groups, make their own arrangements, often with factories or schools, for performance dates and ticket sales, and keep the greater percentage of their earnings.

However, despite the buttressed freedoms in the economy, ideological controls became increasingly strict. Officials began to grow uneasy lest the excitement in the economy lead to "unhealthy tendencies" and "looking toward money in everything." In political study meetings, people were encouraged, on the one hand, to combat leftist opposition to the economic liberalizations, but on the other, to oppose the "rottenness" of "bourgeois thought." A new model for young people to "learn from" was introduced in May 1983, a girl, crippled from birth, named Zhang Haidi. Her example was intended to show people how to overcome their doubts about socialism and become upstanding contributors to the Four Modernizations. When Deng Xiaoping's *Works* were published on July 1, the currently acceptable ideological principles were available in black and white as a focus for "study," and it became clearer what the limits were. The spring campaign against economic crimes, which led into the attack on common criminal behavior of late summer, punished transgressors with execution, long prison terms, or exile to distant labor camps. The year ended with the anti–spiritual pollution movement.

The intellectual liberalization that had accompanied the economic responsibility system in the arts, and the unusually outspoken speeches and articles surrounding the 100th anniversary of the death of Karl Marx in March, were thus followed by one of the worst seasons for intellectual freedom that China had seen in a long time. These were the year's principal events, in sequence:

—Performing artists gained considerable independence of party control. They were permitted to determine their own formats and programs. A wide range of performances emerged, some of them considered "unhealthy" by party leaders.

—New policies gave preferential status to certain high-ranking intellectuals, privileges such as more square footage of housing, telephones, and higher salaries.

—Resistance among leftist middle and lower officials to the policies that favored intellectuals was publicized when a letter from two Hunan University professors protesting their continuing poor treatment received major attention in the *People's Daily*. From February to June, numerous articles describing the plight of intellectuals appeared, and many problems were investigated and rectified. Intellectuals felt encouraged to speak out.

—On the celebration of the 100th anniversary of the death of Karl Marx held on March 13, there was wide discussion of such sensitive questions as Marxist humanism and socialist alienation. Even *Das Kapital* was criticized. Among party ideologists, the climate was extremely liberal.

—Taking heart from these developments, writers and artists resumed expression of humanistic and humanitarian themes, and the denunciation of corruption.

—The economic permissiveness led to a materialistic trend, criticized as "looking toward money in everything." High party leaders involved in economic crimes were arrested.

—In May the new model individual, Zhang Haidi, was introduced to encourage young people to overcome their disillusionment, and on July 1 Deng Xiaoping's *Works*, some of which defined ideological limits, were published. The contract system for performing artists was gradually revoked.

—Beginning in late August, a massive attack on criminals began. By some estimates there were 3,000 to 5,000 executions,[4] all carried out quickly with little prospect of appeal. In some cities, a general nervousness over the numbers of arrests swept the general population, although many sup-

ported the crackdown. Even minor offenders might find
themselves sent off to a distant province for labor reform,
with little prospect of return.

—On October 12 the Central Committee announced a
party rectification to improve the party's image, set to begin
in 1984 and last three years, with Cultural Revolution leftists
as principal targets for expulsion and/or criminal sentencing. At the same time, attention was called to a "per-
missive tendency" which was not to be tolerated.

—Seizing on Deng Xiaoping's mention of laxity on the
Right, party conservatives launched the campaign to eliminate "spiritual pollution" with an October 23 article in the
People's Daily. Leveled against certain writers and artists, and
against theoreticians who spread such notions as socialist
alienation, the movement included among its targets young
people who "mistrust socialism."

The winds of 1983 had blown warm. But during the last
quarter of the year they were very chilly indeed.

"Good" Thought and "Bad"

Freedom of thought has been guaranteed in China's
four constitutions (of 1954, 1975, 1978, and 1982), but in practice such freedom has been limited to those who do not
come in conflict with the party and its policies. The 1982
constitution states that "the exercise by citizens of the
People's Republic of China of their freedoms and rights
may not infringe upon the interests of the state, of society
and of the collective." In other words, only if people love
socialism and uphold Marxism–Leninism–Mao Zedong
Thought, the people's democratic dictatorship, the socialist

road, and the leadership of the party do they have the right to believe as they wish.

Although reforms meant there were more self-employed, in 1983 the vast majority of Chinese working people still belonged to work units, which issued their salaries and the ration coupons without which they would have found it difficult to purchase basic foodstuffs. The unit usually provided housing, and kept personal dossiers on members, which recorded birthplace, ancestry, and political black marks and gold stars dating from entrance to middle school. Each unit had its party leaders and might, depending on its size, be subdivided into smaller party branches. These leaders were charged with influencing, supervising, inspecting, and keeping records on the "thought" of the people in their organizations. Even in units where by 1983 professionals had begun to take over administrative posts, much power was still in the hands of the generally uneducated party cadres.

Political study, which became widespread during the Cultural Revolution, although its origins were earlier, had been in most places reduced from two afternoons a week to one, and in some cities meetings were even less frequent. Political study had usually involved listening to party officials read newspaper articles or party documents transmitted from a higher level; discussing the documents in smaller groups; criticizing oneself if one had thought, spoken, or behaved in ways not in accordance with the spirit of the documents; and summarizing how each person's "thought" had progressed. At times leaders criticized unit members in meetings. It was more serious to be criticized by name, less to be criticized indirectly. Although it was possible to ignore the lecture-style political study sessions (reading novels, knitting, and complaining in low voices were popular ways to pass the time), one was often obliged to express oneself in the smaller groups, which were generally led by group leaders, by members of propaganda committees, or, in schools, by Communist Youth League members. Over the years, people had become adept at presenting themselves as orthodox. Even during periods of relative "looseness," it usually paid to be careful, to stay in the middle of the road and avoid talking as much as possible. All too often, leaders kept track of what people were up to for possible future use, and there was no way to tell whether what was being studied as correct one day would be criticized tomorrow. It was usually best not to support anything too warmly or attack anything too harshly.

In 1983 the study of Chinese Communist Party Document No. 1 varied according to the work unit involved. In factories and performing arts units, such study often meant active discussion of how to apply the "responsibility system." People were required to give their opinions of the new regulations; if some did not understand them, or feared chaos or a loss of security, they were encouraged to express this. In units already practicing the reforms, disagreements were aired and problems dealt with. In universities and schools, where the responsibility system had no direct application, students and teachers listened to documents but usually used discussion time to talk about problems at their own institutions.

Beginning on February 26, 1983, with Premier Zhao Ziyang's television address on the importance of the Five Stresses, Four Beauties, and Three Ardent Loves campaign, political study received new impetus. The Five Stresses and Four Beauties had been announced on February 25, 1981. The Three Ardent Loves were added in March.[1] The movement was an attempt to create a "socialist spiritual civilization" and to rectify the public discourtesy and disorderliness which some saw as a legacy of the anarchy of the Cultural

Revolution. People were exhorted not to spit on the floor, swear, push when boarding buses, and so on. Political study meetings could lead to cleanups of work unit buildings and grounds, to tree and flower planting, or garbage collection. The Three Ardent Loves were, of course, echoes of the Four Basic Principles and were added, presumably, in order to link ethics with patriotism.

The movement to learn from Zhang Haidi was introduced in the May 12, 1983, *People's Daily* with calligraphy written by Deng Xiaoping and Ye Jianying (one of the most senior of high party leaders, now retired). Zhang Haidi was a quite different model from Lei Feng, the selfless, idealized, and emotionally untroubled model People's Liberation Army soldier who preceded her. Zhang was a cripple who had suffered and lost hope during the Cultural Revolution. But she had industriously studied Marxism–Leninism–Mao Zedong Thought: she had struggled with herself, and was now determined to do her best to contribute to the Four Modernizations. She was tailor-made for the disillusioned young, tailor-made to combat the publicly recognized "Three *Xin* Crisis" (of belief in the party, confidence in socialism, and trust of party cadres). She even studied English on her own and enjoyed Western literature. That even China's model individuals were seen as disillusioned and needing renewal of hope shows how widespread the "crisis" was at the time. Often an individual unit's own "Zhang Haidi–style individual" was located and praised.

In late summer, the study of the *Works* of Deng Xiaoping supplanted the movement to learn from Zhang Haidi. Deng's writings are wide-ranging, and work units could select those articles that most closely matched their own situations. The publication of the *Works* brought to an end any fantasies that Deng was a true liberal. The book includes a reference to the Four Basic Principles made as early as

March 1979. Some articles oppose bourgeois liberalism and the Democracy Wall, criticizing those who have doubts about socialism, think capitalism superior, or grovel before foreigners. There are strict articles on corruption and abuses of privilege within the party, and on opposing ultraleftist diehards. The publication of Deng's *Works* appeared to be addressed to conservative leftists and democratic liberals alike. Study of the *Works* did not, of course, leave much room for discussion. People were expected to identify areas of behavior and application of policy inconsistent with Deng's writings, and try to correct them.

Political study in 1983 was not only about domestic questions—another subject for 1983 meetings was the poor U.S.-China relations, caused by the breakdown in textile negotiations, the Hu Na defection, and U.S. demands for payment on certain pre-Liberation railroad bonds. Hu Na's "thought" was bad, the West was said to be wrong to have given her asylum, and so on. Those who admired the United States had to temper their enthusiasm, and informal contacts with foreigners became temporarily more likely to expose people to criticism.

Because the campaign against spiritual pollution of late autumn was defined so vaguely, it did not necessarily touch every political study group directly. In places where the campaign was being implemented, there were varying interpretations and emphases, some of them wild. But, in general, spiritual pollution was taken to mean such things as pornography, including videotapes; materialism ("looking toward money in everything"); doubts about socialism; gambling, smuggling, and other shady activities; and certain ideas in works of literature and art. Leaders of different units stressed one or another of these "pollutions" according to the nature of the units, their own political sympathies, and their perceptions of which way the wind was blowing.

In the early 1980s, in addition to political study, party leaders also used "activists" to supervise people's thought. Activists, generally people very loyal to the party or eager for advancement or favors, were known for making "small reports" to the leaders about unorthodox behavior or comments they had overheard. They were asked to "do thought work" with people who were hesitant to speak out in meetings, who objected to their job assignments, or who were in other ways discontent. "Activists" had become increasingly unpopular over the years, and their numbers had declined. Many saw them as holdovers from Cultural Revolution days. At times pressure was placed on those party members who were not "leaders" to perform similar activist functions—hence the distrust that many had of party members, despite the fact that many party members, too, became disillusioned during the Cultural Revolution. Leaders also learned about individuals' opinions when they applied to join the Communist Youth League or the party, for applicants were required to write "thought reports."

Each middle-school student was responsible for an annual report evaluating his thought for the year, to be placed in his dossier and to remain there for the rest of his life (in recent years, this task has been taken much less seriously). The basic work of molding Chinese minds was thus accomplished long before adulthood, in the kindergartens, schools, and universities. As Minister of Education He Dongcan said on November 28, 1983, "The responsibility of us educators is to train students who support the leadership of the Communist party and wish to serve socialism."[2] Article One of the High School Rules (Trial Draft) stated:

"Ardently love the motherland, support the leadership of the Chinese Communist party and resolve to serve socialism and the people"; Article Two: "Earnestly study Marxism–Leninism–Mao Zedong Thought and gradually establish the proletarian viewpoint, labor viewpoint, mass viewpoint, and dialectic materialist viewpoint."[3] Even toddlers learned to dance and sing in the right political vein. Membership in the political organizations, the Young Pioneers and the Communist Youth League, was early held up as the reward for proper thought and behavior. An additional incentive was the possibility of being honored as a "Three Good Student" (good morals, good grades, good health), becoming a model for one's peers to emulate. Politics classes in everything from Communist party history to Marxism ensured early memorization of right and wrong. For example, middle-school politics classes in Xian studied the *Works* of Deng Xiaoping, "to link politics and class with the party's line and policies, and in this way increase the students' feelings for the party."[4]

In the early 1980s, even in university-level history or philosophy classes foreign ideas were usually mentioned only with a critical eye; Marxism–Leninism–Mao Zedong Thought was the informing viewpoint. Even extracurricular activities taught the proletarian view; "labor," for example, an important component of school life during the Cultural Revolution, was still required in most schools although it often consisted of little more than a day or two of landscaping work per semester. Outside the schools, literature and the arts "engineered" the students' souls, and even entertainment magazines were known to criticize such incorrect ideas as individualism and the worship of foreign things.

Toward the end of 1983, as officials throughout the country hurried to jump onto the bandwagon against spiritual pollution, a series of articles in party newspapers stressed

the importance of "strengthening political thought education work" in the schools and universities. One typical article was published on December 3 in the *People's Daily*:

Qinghua University's party committee's emphasis on carrying out
Marxist-Leninist education of students, on helping students set
up revolutionary outlooks on life, and on opposing spiritual pollution, has received very good results.

For a time, a portion of students numbly worshipped bourgeois civilization, and had doubts about the socialist road. Some
fantasized they could find out from Western bourgeois enlight-
enment scholars the way to cure the country. Facing this situation,
since 1980 Qinghua University has added modern Chinese history
to its politics class to help students see the logic that "Only socialism can save China." Furthermore, they have invited old teachers to tell about their experiences in new and old China, so as to
help students distinguish between fact and fiction. The school
used a semester's political activities, organizing students to study
the "Resolution Concerning Certain Historical Questions of the
Party Since the Establishment of the Country" [the document on
Mao's role] to lead students to sort out for themselves the influence of the bourgeois liberal trend. The school has also started
optional classes in international Communist history and the original works of Marx and Lenin. In the entire school, 170 groups
for the study of Marxism-Leninism have appeared. Over 3,000
students have participated in the Marxist-Leninist study groups
and optional politics classes. To combat the problem of those
students influenced by "free development" thought, who are concerned only for themselves, the school party committee has asked
more than ninety old school friends who have contributed to the
strength of the country to give talks, has organized the students
to go to the countryside and industries and mines for social investigation, has given awards to "Three Good Students," and educated most students in the revolutionary world outlook. . . .

Another important method of opposing spiritual pollution
used in Qinghua has been to help students master revolutionary
literature and art theory, and raise their appreciative abilities. . . .
In order to help students draw a clear line of demarcation between
the noble and the depraved, since 1981 the school has established

classes in "Literature Concepts" and "Selections from Foreign Literature," which use Marxist literature and art views to direct the students' extracurricular reading. It has also established a "Music Concepts" class . . . for carrying out criticisms of unhealthy works, through this slowly increasing the students' interest in art. Many students have brought tapes of unhealthy Taiwan and Hong Kong songs to the recording room, asking that they be re-recorded with noble works.

But what advantage was it to such students or adults to have "good thought"? Until recently, the political cadres made almost all the important decisions that affected the lives of those under them, not only in schools, but in factories, hospitals, and in all other urban work units as well. They controlled salary increases, promotions, job assignments (for students), job transfers, housing allocation, the distribution of certain special ration tickets, and even permission for marriage, divorce, and conceiving a child. One or another of these questions has posed a major headache for almost every urban Chinese. How could anyone afford to antagonize the leaders? It was often not even enough to show oneself ideologically sound. Gifts were often required as well, traditionally liquor and cigarettes, later watches, tape recorders, and even television sets. There was little alternative. If, for example, another unit wished to hire someone, his own unit first had to consent to his departure. If someone wished to apply to a university, his leaders had to consent before he could even sit for the examination, much less leave for school. An entire family might share a single room—the work unit decided whether they got one of the terribly scarce new apartments. Someone might desperately need one of the ration tickets that allowed the purchase of a better-made Shanghai bicycle—again, these were in the hands of the leaders. Many people spent literally every spare fen on gifts, often for years and to little avail because too many others were also competing for the leaders' favor. Some leaders were akin to petty despots, and one of the only hopes of appeal was to go above their heads to *their* leaders, and try to purchase more powerful cooperation. "Good thought" was only the essential beginning.

For someone who did succeed in gaining leaders' confidence, the benefits could be measured not only materially but also in terms of a sense of security and "backing." If, however, a person had "bad thought" or had otherwise managed to incur disfavor, the consequences could be extremely unpleasant. Many of the students who participated in the election movements of the autumn of 1980, for example, later got bad job assignments in impoverished areas far from home, while second-rate students who had cultivated the leaders got plum positions. Some people spent years being victimized by leaders to whom they did not show a sufficiently good "political performance." Thus a person's "thought" had an immediate and important connection with his basic life needs, and in the public arena, at least, there was little possibility of exercising genuine freedom of thought. Far too much was at stake, and the costs of unorthodoxy too great.

Speech and Silence

The Communist party has limited free speech ever since its early days in Yanan. The Yanan Rectification of May 1942 labeled as counterrevolutionaries a number of prominent intellectuals who had criticized the party, including the writers Ding Ling and Xiao Jun. Afterwards, even party members were relatively unwilling to voice dissent. During the Hundred Flowers Movement of 1956, party leaders worked hard to convince people to speak out, but many who were foolish enough to do so were quickly punished in the Anti-rightist Movement of the following year. During the Cultural Revolution, the freedom to criticize some power holders was circumscribed within pro-Mao fanaticism. Although many of the pent-up frustrations of the Chinese people were voiced, the Cultural Revolution became a kind of mass insanity unleashed and exploited by the ultra-leftists in their struggle for power. The majority of the millions of people persecuted during that period were victimized not for crimes but for what they had said or believed.

When the 1978 constitution guaranteed freedom of speech, this was boldly and literally interpreted by democratic activists as a sign that they might speak out. But in March 1979 the Beijing and Shanghai Municipal Party Committees passed a "Public Announcement on the Protection of Social Discipline," and the crackdown on "counterrevolutionaries" began. (This "Public Announcement" had gone through no legal enactment procedure.) In January the Central Committee withdrew the "Four Greats," the guarantees of free expression that included the right to put up big character posters and hold public debates.[1] On April 10 a 1951 law on guarding "state secrets" was republished. These "secrets" were only vaguely defined and no limit on punishments was specified. Party leaders at all levels were urged to make the prevention of leaks their "constant task"; this cast a pall on free speech, especially in dealings with foreigners. The 1982 constitution institutionalized the cautionary atmosphere with its mention of the Four Basic Principles in its preamble.

During the early 1980s, four levels of sanctions were employed against those who violated taboos on speech: criminal, subcriminal, disciplinary, and informal.[2] The gravest of these was applied against those said to have committed "counterrevolutionary crimes of speech." Wei Jingsheng and a minority of democratic activists were in this category. The severity of Wei's fifteen-year sentence frightened other activists, and by late 1980 fewer and fewer people were willing to run the risks of the organized activities that could lead to such accusations, particularly the giving of speeches and the publication of unofficial magazines. After the arrests of democratic election movement activists in the spring of 1981, virtually no one was willing to do such things.

Still common, however, were arrests for overstepping the second level of limits on free speech, which involved such matters as putting up posters or expressing strong dissent in political study meetings. The punishment for this type of behavior was the commonly used "labor reform"—normal sentence, three years. No court procedures were necessary for this level of arrest. The local Public Security Bureau could simply send away anyone it considered dangerous, and the leaders of work units could request that a difficult employee or student be dealt with in this way. This was the fate of many of the Democracy Wall activists and university election movement activists; only a handful were given criminal sentences.

There were labor camps throughout China, but people arrested in the big cities were often sent to the huge camps in China's deserted West, particularly in Qinghai and Xinjiang Provinces. Although technically not criminals or "enemies of the state," the internees generally lived together with ordinary criminals and spent their days in the same hard labor. Most frightening for these people was that their residence cards, which gave them the right to get ration coupons and hence the ability to purchase staple foods, were transferred with them to the camps. Even if they were released, it was often impossible for them to return to their home cities. Labor reform was the most efficient way to deal with all kinds of offenders, including ordinary petty thieves, gamblers, and "dangerous elements." During the August–October 1983 crime sweep-up, enormous numbers were sent away to the labor camps—the U.S. State Department estimates tens of thousands, with more than 100,000 total population in the camps.[3]

The third level of sanctions against crimes of speech were the disciplinary measures taken by the leaders of a work unit or, in the case of an important artist, writer, or publisher, by the Central Committee itself. These measures were often used against those who showed an open "lack of confidence in the party," were "dissatisfied with reality," or perhaps demonstrated "excessive individualism." The main punishment was public criticism in political study meetings or over the unit's loudspeaker, criticism often softened by the use of the word "comrade" or even by omitting the offender's name entirely. Such methods were an attempt to shame the offender by enlisting the disapproval of friends and colleagues, and to frighten him with the threat of isolation; they also served as a warning to other unit members against doing the same thing. It was generally necessary for the offender to write a self-criticism. This went into his dossier, together with a record of his actions and attitudes. If the offense was deemed particularly serious, a transfer to another position or even to another unit, perhaps in another city, could sometimes be the outcome.

An example of this level of sanction comes from the October 30, 1983, *People's Daily*. In Wuhan University, the seven literary clubs and nineteen student magazines were found to be printing articles that revealed suspicion of socialism, lack of confidence in the party, and so on. The heads of these groups and magazines, although legitimate leaders of the party-supported Student Committee, were publicly crit-

icized; the need for "firmer leadership" and strict examination of articles before publication was announced; and some
of the student leaders lost their positions. This was a major
incident. The usual criticisms during political study had,
however, lost much of their force over the years. In the
universities and factories especially, where young people
predominated, the attitudes of the offenders were often
shared by the audience listening to the criticisms. The offenders were sometimes openly indifferent to what was
being said about them, while there was general public
amusement at the charges. In the early 1980s, it was only
when job assignment time neared in the universities that
students began to reconsider the importance of what the
leaders thought of them.

A fourth level of sanctions, informal ones, were directed
against those who had not done anything worthy of public
criticism but who were considered to have "bad thought,"
who liked to complain, who were guilty of absenteeism or
cutting classes, and so on. Here the punishments were unspoken, but they could be fearsome nonetheless—bad job
assignments, refusals of various permissions, and the many
other punishments already mentioned. When, however,
nearly all the members of a work unit shared the same cyn-
ical attitudes, even these sanctions lost much of their power.

The question of freedom of speech is, of course, inseparable
from the question of freedom *not* to speak. During the
Hundred Flowers Movement, there was still some possibility of remaining silent, but during the Cultural Revolution,
it became incumbent upon everyone (except those who had
lost their civil and political rights) to "express an attitude"
during meetings. Particularly during the early period of the
Cultural Revolution, it was impossible to remain unin-
volved if one did not wish to be called a counterrevolution-

ary for one's silence. However, speaking out was almost as dangerous, since policies were always changing and it was never clear when a viewpoint was truly safe. People learned during that period to protect themselves by holding back to see what others would say, and then imitating them. Fear of being wrong was a powerful impetus toward ideological conformity. People also learned how to memorize what newspapers and documents said, and how to speak in the same spirit when called upon in public situations. Thus the official written materials transmitted at a certain time came gradually to determine the language used all over the country. The 1983 newspaper stories about Zhang Haidi, for example, told people what they should say they had learned from her, and there was thus an extraordinary unity in the "lessons" taught in schools, factories, the army, and so on, all over China. The materials announcing the 1984 party rectification included a required-reading list for the entire country. The language and concepts of those works thus told people how to present themselves in public situations.

Although compulsory "expressions of attitude" have become less frequent in recent years, they were still common in the early 1980s. In such situations, people had to hide their real feelings, even to speak against others they have had no wish to harm. During the campaign against spiritual pollution, for example, meetings were held in local branches of arts committees, in publications units and performing troupes to discuss and criticize problematic works. A number of well-known writers and intellectuals willing to speak out for party policies, such as the long-persecuted Ding Ling, and Zhang Kejia, an old friend of Mao, did so, but the party also found it useful to use people who were themselves considered guilty of "wrong tendencies" as critics. For example, the novelist Zhang Xiaotian, who was severely criticized for his unacceptably humanistic 1982 work, Sparse

Prairie Grasses (*Lili Yuanshang Cao*), was obliged to write a self-criticism after his work had been attacked, saying that he had forgotten that as a party member it was his responsibility to speak for the party, that his level of Marxism–Leninism–Mao Zedong Thought was inadequate, and so on. What was notable about that particular self-criticism was that Zhang had earlier written to friends saying he was unafraid of trouble, that in order to express what he believed, he would take any consequences. That letter and his public statement read as if they were by two entirely different people. It is obvious that Zhang had little choice about whether to speak out and what to say.

At times, the prudent person did not wait to be forced to speak out—he tried to gauge what was correct and say it so as not to be accused of lagging. This guessing game has been played by virtually every Chinese who has had to participate in political study. Sometimes, of course, a wrong estimation could be troublesome. Many, for example, were overenthusiastic during the campaign to "liberate thought" in 1980. The need to express an attitude early could also lead to misinterpretations of the intentions behind a newly issued article or document.

The knee-jerk reaction of middle- and lower-level cadres to the first mention of the need to combat spiritual pollution exemplifies this. When the newspapers first mentioned the question in October 1983, it was in general terms without specified targets. It was announced that a meeting would be scheduled in 1984 to discuss the question. However, reactions were quicker on lower levels than at the top, as officials in various provinces and work units rushed to avoid being left behind. The result was that spiritual pollution was interpreted in broad and inconsistent terms. This tendency on the part of officials to rush to support leftist policies and directives had become fundamental to leaders' social psychology, a residue of the Cultural Revolution and an indication of how strong leftism remained in China.

The lack of freedom not to speak affected interpersonal relations adversely. Especially in the early years after the Cultural Revolution, it was often difficult for people to trust anyone but a few close friends and relatives. It was difficult to judge what people's beliefs really were, since they might be speaking in certain ways only to protect themselves. There was always the danger that what you said might be used against you, either immediately, as a way of currying favor with the leaders, or in the future, as a shift in the political current made betrayal a means of survival. The fact that most people spent their entire lives in one work unit, and thus had to consider that they would always have to deal with the same co-workers, made them even more careful. There was a saying, "Three together speak falsehoods, two together curse the leaders." It reflected the fear of being reported on if there was a corroborating witness.

If something someone did or said reached the ears of the leaders, he had to deal with his suspicions of who was responsible for ratting, possibly souring his relations with everyone. It is only natural, then, that people often preferred not to give others power over them by talking about sensitive questions. They mastered the art of speaking charmingly about safe subjects such as food, dialect differences, and weather. Even in more recent years, they have tended to avoid speaking about politics, rarely even asking each other about their families. A new acquaintance's work unit, however, is usually ascertained almost immediately; a common greeting is, "Where are you going?" In Chinese, no word for "privacy" exists.

In the years following the Cultural Revolution, caution in speech became such an instinctive custom that the admonition to "be careful what you say" became a sign of solicitous concern for another person. Reticence was also common even among students studying abroad, who had no way of knowing who among their fellow scholars might be reporting to the local consulate on their speech and behavior. In 1984 one visiting scholar in the U.S. received a letter from his mother reminding him to uphold the Four Basic Principles, while another routinely asked friends to meet him in private for fear that he might be overheard. Despite the fact that these people were living temporarily in an open society, their self-protective instincts were almost the same as if they were still living in China.

Such caution was often quite unnecessary since, after all, Cultural Revolution days were over. The nervousness, the lowering of the voice and the quick look around, the pat on the shoulder and the confidential "don't tell anyone": these had become the habitual gestures of a nation still recovering from a nightmare.

Political Participation and Protest

Limitations on free speech inevitably affected the few opportunities Chinese had for political participation. In general, in the early 1980s they had two ways to make their views known: first, through the ritualistic local elections; and second, through several routes for appeal or protest.

Local elections were for representatives to county-level People's Congresses; delegates were then chosen by these representatives for district-level congresses, and on up to provincial and national levels. Such delegates had little or no power, since real power in China was in the hands of the party rather than in the National People's Congress, which still functioned largely as a source of suggestions and rubber stamping. Elections of delegates, according to the 1979 law which established them, were to be held every four years. Those held in some university districts in the autumn of 1980 were those which got out of hand, with self-appointed candidates, platforms, and speeches. (A second round of elections was held in 1984.)

In the vast majority of election districts, the 1980 elections were simply formalities for legitimating the party, enlisting a sense of investment and involvement by the voters, and gaining their cooperation. Votes were taken at people's work units, which were divided into districts according to geographical location. The party committees in each unit administered the elections. Most voters understood that the candidates were to be party-selected, and that the outcomes were essentially predetermined. They took little interest in the voting, some even writing "pig" or "dog" on their ballots to show they knew how irrelevant their votes were.

(In 1984 even the universities were quiet. College students were no longer members of the "lost" Red Guard generation whose experiences had disillusioned and freed them to analyze China comparatively independently. Rather, they were young people fresh out of middle school, students who had not experienced the Cultural Revolution directly and who had little knowledge of it because of the moratorium the party had imposed on the subject in art, literature, and film. The new generation was far more interested in material advancement than in thinking about the roots of China's troubles. The elections passed almost unnoticed, another routine item on the political study agenda.)

A far more useful, if risky, way for people to express their views was through appeals, which included those to the various levels of Discipline Inspection Committees, to the legal system, and to the newspapers. The right to appeal was guaranteed in the 1982 constitution: citizens could "make to relevant state organs, complaints and charges against, or exposures of, any state organ or functionary for violation of the law or dereliction of duty." The Discipline Inspection Committees (or Groups, depending on level) existed at all strata of the Chinese bureaucracy. They were established in 1979, primarily to deal with the vast number of "wrong decisions" handed down during the Cultural Revolution. According to a report in the October 2, 1983, *People's Daily*, in 1982 such organs received 7,600,000 letters and 2,630,000 requests in person to deal with injustices. If the "wrong decision" involved legal sentencing to prison or execution (rather than, say, "labeling" as a counterrevolutionary or rightist), the appeal was to the courts, the second locus for appeal. According to a January 13, 1983, *People's Daily* report, from October 1981 to September 1982 local courts dealt with 180,600 cases, while the Supreme Court dealt with an additional 124,200 and interviewed 30,000 people. A third method of appeal was to write to or visit the newspapers. Every newspaper had a "letters and visits" office. Sometimes the major newspapers such as the *People's Daily* had an even greater ability to resolve problems than the Discipline Inspection Committees or the courts. After an account of abuse or injustice appeared in the newspapers, Discipline Inspection Committees and courts were far more likely to pay attention to it. Sometimes inspection committee and court officials even wrote letters to the newspapers themselves if they were having difficulty resolving a problem because of noncooperation or pressure from cadres involved in the case.

However, since the newspapers expressed the views of top party officials, they were likely to print something only if it happened to suit the needs of the current political struggle. A problem would often be highlighted in order to shore up a political faction, depending upon which faction controlled the paper. (The *People's Daily* has generally been controlled by reformers since soon after Deng's return to power in 1977, while *Red Flag* [*Hongqi*] has been the voice of the more orthodox group.)

Two Hunan University professors whose letter protesting the treatment of intellectuals by local party leaders was published in the February 23, 1983, *People's Daily* were very lucky. Leftist Hunan officials who were still dragging their feet in "overturning the sentences" of persecuted intellectuals were precisely the kind of people that the Deng faction was trying to weed out. Hunan was already notorious for its Maoism (it is Mao's home province): Mao's immediate successor Hua Guofeng ("With you in command, my heart is at ease") had been first party secretary there during the Cultural Revolution; the current party secretary, Mao Zhiyong, an old "whateverist," is said to have been Hua's personal appointee. The large number of articles in party newspapers on the situation in Hunan University from February to June 1983 reflected this high-level power struggle.

However, the letter alone did not solve the problem. Initial excitement and gratitude toward the two professors for daring to speak out gave way to disheartenment and renewed caution as investigating teams and classes for party leaders yielded few results. According to a May 17 *People's Daily* article, 995 people attached to the university wanted to have official judgments about their political histories rechecked, and one had written more than eighty letters, to little avail. The depth of leftist oppression of intellectuals was reflected in the discouragement they expressed to the investigators, who reported: "They worry that the problems will not be fundamentally solved and that things will be done perfunctorily. Their minds are again laden with doubts and fears. Some teachers told us about their bitter experience, but the following day declared what they had said to be invalid." According to the May 21 *Guangming Daily*, a special organ set up by the Hunan Provincial Party Committee to inspect the implementation of the policies toward intellectuals received 1,700 to 1,800 letters in about a month. Furthermore, letters were received from many other institutions, not only in Hunan but all over the country, protesting mistreatment of intellectuals. Publication of such letters drew attention to the plight of intellectuals, but this was far from sufficient. Even in Hunan University, where national concern for the problem could have been expected to bring speedy resolution, local resistance was enormous and obstacles great.

Despite the existence of the officially established mechanisms for appeal, in the early 1980s most Chinese still hesitated to use them. One reason was that the odds were great that their appeals would not receive attention and that even if they did, the problem might not be solved; another was that there was considerable danger that their appeals would backfire and bring them even more trouble. The appeals usually ended up being transmitted back to the local work units, where, often enough, the officials charged with dealing with the cases had close relationships with the leaders being accused.

The discipline inspection committee system worked as follows: a person with a grievance was supposed to write to his own unit's discipline inspection office. If he feared he would not get a fair hearing there, he could write to a higher office. If he was in an educational unit, for example, this would be the discipline inspection committee of the municipal education section of the provincial education department, or even of the Ministry of Education in Beijing. However, the chances were overwhelming that unless an important leader took an unusual interest in the case, these higher offices would not make a judgment or an investigation but would simply affix a stamp to the supplicant's letter and write an order for the next lower office to deal with the matter. And so on down the ranks until the appeal returned to the original work unit. Since many of the leaders of a given unit were hired by the unit's higher-ups, and since in any case the people adjacent to one another in the bureaucratic hierarchy usually had good relationships warmed with gifts and favors, the supplicant was usually out of luck. He might even be criticized for not following normal procedures and trying to go over the heads of local administrators, and be still further victimized.

Such results are related to the question of privacy of correspondence. Although in the early 1980s personal letters were rarely examined (those to people being watched by the Public Security Bureau and of some from abroad were exceptions), letters of appeal were not, ultimately, private. Another source of nervousness about putting things in writing was memories of the Cultural Revolution, when letters and diaries had been routinely used as evidence to prove people guilty of counterrevolutionary ideas. Many people preferred to make their appeals in person, avoiding written evidence that could be used against them. Telephones in China were still very poor in quality, and conversations could easily be overheard by zealous work unit operators. But appeals in person were also hard, for individuals were shy about going to a new place and stating their business, and the generally unsympathetic attitudes of many urban office workers were no encouragement. (Such considerations also discouraged people from going through the legal system.) The vast majority of those with grievances, therefore, tended to suffer in silence. Indeed, the ability to bear suffering had become a national character trait of which the Chinese were, perhaps mistakenly, proud.

In practice, the method of redressing wrongs most commonly used was "the back door." Through gifts and favors, a good relationship was established with leaders higher up than the leader or leaders responsible for the abuse, so that these might bring pressure to bear on the victim's behalf. The other possibility was to try to make connections with someone who could hand carry a letter to a higher leader of his acquaintance, in the hope that the personal contact might induce the leader to intercede.

Silent protests, such as absenteeism or a noncooperative attitude, were also used with occasional success, although they were risky. For example, a teacher once let it be known that he would be on sick leave until his family got a new apartment assignment—they got their extra room. But, according to a December 20, 1983, *People's Daily* report, when six out of the 400 students from Shanghai who disliked their job assignments refused to show up, they were made examples of for others. They were criticized as individualists who opposed the party, and their rights to work were revoked forever. The remaining 394, according to a March 3, 1984, report, went to work [1]

No discussion of freedom of speech in early 1980s China would be complete without a description of the work team system, whereby an investigative group was sent from a higher level to gather information on the situation at a lower one. (It is still commonly used today.) While the team was present, people were encouraged to speak to its members in confidence, and a certain amount of frankness was often possible. The work team system was widely used, for example, in 1983 during the "reform of leadership" designed to shake up the bureaucracy, bring in more qualified people, and get rid of some of the leftists.[2] At each level of leadership change, work teams tried to ascertain which of the current officials, in the opinions of the masses, were doing a good job, which were not, and who would be welcomed as replacements. Of course, the masses' opinions were only part of the information used during the shakeups, and there was no guarantee that they were considered at all. However, such investigations did seem to pose some obstacles to the appointments of very unpopular leaders. (The 1983 reforms in the leadership, incidentally, were not always successful, precisely because of the net of relationships described above. New leaders came in without the support of the officials below them and were unable to function well. There were even cases of leadership changes being rescinded for this reason.)

In sum, freedom of speech in China in the early 1980s was restricted through various levels of sanctions, while the appeals process, too, was limited and risky. People had learned that it was better to put up with an unjust situation than to rock the boat, although there were some outstanding exceptions.

Religion and the Drive
Against Superstition

Since the restoration in 1979 of "freedom of religious belief," there has been a tremendous reflorescence of religious activity in China. The 1982 constitution specifies that people may not be forced to believe or disbelieve, or be discriminated against because of religious beliefs. However, in the early 1980s this freedom was circumscribed by restrictions in interactions with foreign religious groups seen as threatening to the party's supremacy, by informal pressures on believers by the leaders of some work units, by prohibi-

tions against proselytizing, and by a distinction made between religion and superstition (the latter was forbidden).
The constitution interdicts activities that "disrupt social order, harm the health of citizens, or interfere with the country's education system."[1] Furthermore, religious freedom
was limited to those over the age of eighteen. Despite these
limits, the situation for organized religion was remarkably
good, in view of the fact that during the Cultural Revolution the Gang of Four proclaimed that they had eradicated
religion completely (an irony, since Mao worship was akin
to religious fanaticism).

According to Document No. 19, "Communiqué on the
Basic Viewpoint and Basic Policy on the Religious Question During Our Country's Socialist Period,"[2] published
March 31, 1982, China then had ten million believers in Islam,[3] three million Catholics, and three million Protestants;
virtually all the Tibetan, Mongolian, and Dai minorities
were Buddhist or Lamaist, while millions of Han (ethnic
Chinese) were influenced by Buddhism or Daoism. There
were more than 59,000 religious professionals, 27,000 of
whom were Buddhist and Lamaist monks and nuns; the
remainder included over 2,600 Daoists, 20,000 Islamic leaders, more than 3,400 Catholic priests, and more than 5,900
Protestant ministers. There were 30,000 sites for religious
activity (down from 100,000 just after Liberation[4]), and
eight organized religious associations representing four religions: Christianity, Buddhism, Islam, and Daoism.

To the ex–Red Guard generation, Mao was like a god.
After he died, both literally and as a spiritual leader, these
young people began looking for a substitute to fill their
emptiness. They often had more curiosity about Western
religions than about Chinese Buddhism or Daoism, although in Guangdong and Fujian Provinces the Buddha of

Wealth made a major comeback. Tourists were often surprised to be asked for gifts of Bibles and religious materials. A belief in fate, metaphysical if not exactly religious, was widespread, perhaps because Chinese, who had little control over their own lives, usually had to accept the hand life dealt them.

Restoration of religious sites was carried out all over China, although a shortage continued, since many temples, churches, and mosques were turned into factories, warehouses, and residential units during the Cultural Revolution. (There was also a shortage of religious leaders, but young people were being trained.) According to Document No. 19, "Famous mosques, temples, and churches that make a large impression domestically and internationally and have a large value as historical monuments must, as much as circumstances permit, be gradually restored."[5] The document states that it is forbidden to rebuild temples or churches with nongovernment funds, and that restoration must take place under the party's supervision: "Aside from those that have Chinese Communist party permission and funding, other funds or materials are not to be utilized, and the preventing of the restoration of temples in peasant villages needs special attention."[6]

This clause indicates how widespread was peasant interest in such temples, and the potential for abuses by people wishing to take advantage of this enthusiasm. According to 1983 Fujian Province reports, sorcerers had reappeared in number, in one case encouraging peasants to rebuild a temple with 20,000 yuan (now about 6,400 dollars) originally donated by overseas Chinese to bring electricity to the village. Another report said that a sorcerer was able to build a twenty-room house at a cost of from 20,000 to 30,000 yuan (about 6,400 to 9,600 dollars) with his recent earnings.[7]

In the *Washington Post* in 1984, Michael Weisskopf cited incidences of suicides induced by the promise of immortality, occult wedding ceremonies, and murders to exorcise evil spirits. Hainan Island peasants destroyed $300,000 worth of geological equipment because they thought the offshore oil drilling had angered local spirits, and officials based important commune decisions on "auspicious days" selected by fortune-tellers. "Patriarchal clans, waving banners and green paper dragons, clash in disputes over ancestral grave sites," Weisskopf wrote. "Young men posing as born-again emperors ravish village maidens."[8]

Perhaps the revival of sorcery explains why the party grew increasingly concerned in 1983 to differentiate between religion and superstition. A *Guangming Daily* article[9] called superstition such things as:

> . . . telling fortunes by using the eight diagrams, feeling a person's bones and looking at his appearance to forecast his future, practicing geomancy, reading horoscopes in search of an elixir of life, driving away ghosts to cure illnesses, planchette-writing, offering sacrifices to gods, begging gods to bestow children on people, offering prayers to gods to ward off calamities and to ask for rain, and so on.

The article went on to say that such practices "not only corrode the ideology of the people, but also sabotage production, disturb the social order, and even endanger people's lives." However, it is worth pointing out that some traditional Buddhist and Daoist practices were attacked as superstitions, while a number of witchcraftlike practices were performed unchecked in the name of religious freedom. The distinction was not, apparently, as clear-cut as policy makers might have wished.

The question of religious freedom was particularly sensitive since it was often bound up in the comparative satisfaction or dissatisfaction of ethnic minority nationalities living under Han Chinese rule. (The fifty-four identified non-Han ethnic groups in China occupy about half the land, including most of the border areas.) It was in China's interest to give these people religious freedom, since China needed stability, unification, and strong borders. However, some religions practiced by minority peoples once had extensive political functions that could rival party supremacy. When such functions came to be seen as without threat, they were permitted; the Dai people along the Burmese border, for example, have been allowed to use some of their traditional religious structure in their political life. But because for Tibetans (and, to a lesser degree, for Muslims and some of the northwestern minorities) religious beliefs have traditionally carried strong nationalistic feelings, China's record on religious freedom in Tibet was by far the worst. Tibetan activists overseas believe, for example, that the autumn 1983 crime crackdown was used to stifle political dissent, and they claim that five hundred ethnic Tibetans were arrested, thirty-four monks among them, and five political dissidents executed.[10] (China has denied that the executions were politically motivated.) In the early 1980s, the situation for Muslims improved. It became easier for them to get permission to visit Mecca, for example, and the thirtieth anniversary of the founding of the Chinese Muslim organization was celebrated with some fanfare in May 1983.

The single Western religious group that had the greatest difficulty under party rule were the Roman Catholics. Document No. 19 states, "There are counterrevolutionary influences from international religions, especially imperialistic religious influences, including the 'meetings with emissaries' of the Vatican and Protestant religions, who also make efforts to take advantage of various opportunities to launch infiltration activities, and 'return to the China mainland.'"[11]

The maintenance of ties with the Vatican was particularly unacceptable, not only because Rome's authority seemed threatening to Communist supremacy but also because of the Roman Catholic church's traditionally pro-Taiwan stance. The Pope's anti–birth control position was also exceedingly unwelcome in China. In March 1983 four elderly priests received prison terms of up to fifteen years for "colluding with foreign countries, endangering the sovereignty and security of the motherland, collecting intelligence reports, fabricating rumors, and carrying out incitement."[12] One, Bishop Gong Pinmei, was in prison from 1955, with a brief release during 1978 and 1979, to the time of his death early in 1984; another was released in Shanghai in 1985 after he renounced ties to Rome. Some underground groups of Catholics loyal to the Vatican held services in private homes. According to the State Department's 1983 Country Report, "Government efforts against 'house churches' continued in 1983. There were unconfirmed reports of arrests of 30 'house church' leaders in central China, 100 Christians in Henan Province, a number of Christians in Shaanxi Province, and two ethnic Koreans active in the evangelical church movement in Shanghai."[13]

In the early 1980s, party members were strictly forbidden to hold religious beliefs or participate in religious activities, although exceptions were made for minority nationality party members. (One young ethnic Chinese who became a monk lost his party membership.) Also excepted were Han party members working in minority areas, who needed to participate in festivals and ceremonies with religious coloring in order to avoid becoming isolated from the local people.

Leftist leaders in particular tended to look unfavorably on Western religions since these retained, for many of them, associations with the Western imperialism of pre-Liberation days. Some older Christians, many of whom received their educations in missionary schools, were victimized particularly harshly during the Cultural Revolution and regained their social status very late. Young believers, too, were often pressured by their leaders, and were regarded as having "bad thought," especially if they attended religious services. They sometimes received poor job assignments or were in other ways the objects of discrimination.

After the movement to eradicate spiritual pollution began, there was considerable anxiety abroad that religion would become a target. However, the Chinese government moved quickly to allay such fears, because of its concern both for its image overseas and for peace in its border areas. Soon after the two-week visit to China of the Archbishop of Canterbury, Robert Runcie, in early December 1983, the *People's Daily* published an article headed, "Religion and Spiritual Pollution Are Two Different Things; Our Open-door Policy Is an Established National Policy."[14] In reporting a conversation between the archbishop and National Chairman Li Xiannian, the article clearly stated that the spiritual pollution campaign was directed at theory, the arts, and pornography; religion was under legal protection. It is quite possible, however, that some persecution of those who held religious beliefs arose in connection with the campaign.

In considering the question of religious freedom in China it is important to remember that China's pre-Communist religious traditions were not very strong. Confucianism, the dominant ideology, is a moral philosophy rather than a religion. Buddhism and Daoism, especially the latter, thrived primarily as folk religions, with generous complements of deities, ghosts, and fairies. Ancestor worship, an extension of Confucianism, was as close to religion as many Chinese came. Therefore, the Communist suppression of religion during the Cultural Revolution and its later slightly disapproving neutrality toward it must not be seen as a grave hardship for the majority of the Chinese people (unlike the situation in Poland, for example). For the minority of Han believers and for the ethnic minorities, however, times have often been extremely difficult, and for those groups whose beliefs are seen as conflicting with the party and socialism, conditions are unlikely to improve much in the future.

The Arts

Relative liberalization was followed, in the last quarter of 1983, by the most severe crackdown on artistic freedom since the fall of the Gang of Four. That year, literature and the arts followed the pattern in the country as a whole, with comparative looseness in the early months followed by increasing tightness, climaxing in the campaign against spiritual pollution. In the stage arts, the early relaxation was due largely to the fact that economic reforms were widely applied for the first time to performing units, giving individuals greater control over what they put on stage, and an incentive to perform more frequently and in situations arranged without party management. In literary and art circles, there were once again discussions of modernism, humanism, and humanitarianism, encouraged in part by the outspoken atmosphere surrounding the 100th anniversary in March of the death of Karl Marx, when articles were published discussing such sensitive questions as Marxist humanism and socialist alienation. Even General Party Secretary Hu Yaobang spoke out for the role of intellectuals.

Although the contract (*chengbao*) system in the arts had been practiced experimentally in some units in 1982, it re-

ceived widespread encouragement from the Ministry of
Culture in the beginning of 1983. The system was an extension of earlier reforms which made an individual troupe or
factory responsible for at least part of its own upkeep. In
some troupes, however, because expenses were so high,
money was lost every time a performance was given, so the
reforms meant that there was good reason to put on fewer
shows. By the extended reforms, however, artists could
form small performing teams and, managing themselves,
arrange performances as best they could—in factories,
schools, neighborhoods, even in the countryside. They
could divide most of their earnings among themselves, turning the rest over to their mother troupes. They still earned
their basic government salaries and enjoyed benefits such as
medical and child-care supplements, but they no longer
earned the extra income they had been paid when they were
on tour with the troupe.

In Hunan Province, performers told us they were not
obligated to form teams and could elect to stay home and
do nothing. In the Hunan Song and Dance Troupe, out of
251 members about 100 elected to participate in the contract
system, dividing themselves into three teams. Their experiences are a fascinating example of the difficulties encountered when people accustomed to socialist guarantees are
suddenly forced to fend for themselves as if under a capitalist system.[1] They complained that they were used to being
met at the train station, taken to hotels where rooms had
been preassigned, having regular meal times, times for rest-
ing, for getting up, for rehearsal. And they were used to
knowing they would receive their thirty fen for performing
and eighty fen for being away from home on tour, no matter
whether there were two people or a thousand in the audience. Now for the first time they worried about whether
their shows would be popular, about how to sell tickets,

save money on hotels (they said they often slept in the theaters), and find a place to eat.

The Hunan Song and Dance Troupe earned very little money during the contract experiment (the members of one group, only six yuan apiece for the two performances they were able to put on), but members of other troupes more popular with audiences earned much more. In the Hunan Acrobatic Troupe, for example, each performer earned over five hundred yuan. In Hebei Province, one team of traditional *quyi* (folk story telling) performers had sixty-seven shows in three months, another forty-eight.[2] According to the March 1983 issue of *Drama Bulletin* (*Xiju Bao*), all provinces except a few outlying ones had put the contract system into effect, one Beijing Opera team earning 270,000 yuan within sixteen months, or 28,000 yuan after expenses. It had saved the country 100,000 yuan (presumably in costumes, transportation, and other costs). In addition to their monthly salaries, performers received over fifty yuan each.[3]

Performing artists were not the only ones to use the contract system. The Shanghai Writers' Association launched a plan whereby the eight professional writers on salary with the association became project supervisors. Younger writers employed by magazines, factories, and schools were encouraged to make writing proposals to them. If their applications were accepted, the Writers' Association would request leaves of absence from their units on their behalf, taking the responsibility of issuing them their salaries for the period, so that they could spend all their time on writing. If writers produced nothing during their first year, however, they would have to return to their work units.[4]

Under the contract system, all kinds of new problems emerged. In the Hunan Song and Dance Troupe, one leading singer demanded a greater share of the take than the rest. Set designers wanted to be able to participate and were angry if, as an economy, no sets were used, or if sets they had made under the old system were used but they were not recompensed. Dancers found it strenuous to perform so frequently, and to many, the uncertainty of the new system was less attractive than the old "iron rice bowl," despite the opportunity to make more money. When, in March, Hunan Song and Dance Troupe performers were told they would have to go on a long-term contract system under which the unit would no longer provide medical and child-care supplements, most did not wish to take the risk, primarily because their product was not sufficiently attractive to audiences.[5] Many of the acrobats, however, with their more popular product, continued with the experiment, and made plenty of money up until the time the contract system was revoked a few months later in July.

From the party's point of view, the problems that arose under the system were of a different nature. It is true that during the first few months of 1983 there were a tremendous number of performances and it could thus be said that ordinary people's cultural lives became, quite suddenly, much richer. However, there were also "unhealthy tendencies." For example, the newly formed Hunan Province Performance Company (*Hunan Sheng Yanchu Gongsi*) invited a number of famous movie stars to appear in the Provincial Sports Commission stadium for large sums—some said fifty yuan a performance for each of them—and sold tickets at the very high price of six yuan. However, the movie stars did not really have any talents they could use in that format. Some sang a little, badly; others danced a little, also badly. The audience was furious and felt they had been cheated. The commercial exploitation of celebrities (the emergence of celebrities was in itself a troubling, nonsocialistic phenomenon) was one problem cited as a negative outgrowth of the contract system in the arts.

Another problem was the performance styles that many troupes adopted to sell more tickets. Some performers, for example, began wearing sexy clothes: audiences were said to like them *lou, tou, guai*, "revealing, transparent, and strange." Singers used the crooning styles typical of Hong Kong and Taiwan pop stars, holding microphones in their hands and moving all over the stage instead of standing in one place with revolutionary dignity, their arms at their sides. The songs they sang were "unhealthy" ones about love and dreams. To sell tickets in the countryside, opera troupes put on shows about ghosts and demons—traditional tales criticized by the party because they were "superstitious." Such problems were not seriously attacked until mid-summer, however, when the contract system in the arts was being revoked in most provinces.

As it was in the performance arts, the early part of 1983 was a lively time in art theory. The authoritative *Literature and Art Bulletin*, for example, published numerous articles on modern Western literature and its relationship to the development of Chinese literature, posing questions about whether Western literature should guide future developments in Chinese literature, whether the tradition of revolutionary literature was still viable, and whether new writing techniques were necessary or the traditional ones were sufficient. Many of the articles encouraged a break with tradition and an exploration of what Western literature had to offer Chinese writers, both in terms of content and technique. Some, trying to tie Western literature to the modernization campaign, compared the socialist literary tradition to an obsolete steam engine: China, they said, needed to enter the electronic age.

At the end of January 1983, a scholarly conference was held in Beijing by three national-level magazines: *Literary*

Review (*Wenxue Pinglun*), *Literature and Art Bulletin*, and
Literature and Art Research (*Wenyi Yanjiu*). The subject was
"Humanism and Humanitarianism in Our Modern National Literature."[6] Many participants asserted their belief
in the importance of using humanistic themes in literature,
tying such matters to the "liberation of thought" movement. Advocates of humanism (*renxing*) spoke against the
"revolutionary" overemphasis on class relationships. They
said that a "good" character could also have bad characteristics (a party leader did not have to be perfect), while a
"bad" character, a hoodlum for example, could also have
good qualities. Proponents of humanitarianism (*rendao-
zhuyi*) claimed that literature should reflect people's ordinary lives, their loves, friendships, and families, their ideals
and their setbacks. Thus advocates of humanism and humanitarianism in literature suggested that human beings
should be portrayed in greater complexity than they had
been—a marked deviation from the basic tenet of socialist
realism that characters should represent types (*dianxing*)
rather than individuals.

Discussion in the theoretical world reached its climax
around the commemoration of the death of Marx on March
13, 1983. Liberal party theorists, the most famous of whom
was the veteran cultural official Zhou Yang, who later became a major target during the campaign against spiritual
pollution, made speeches and wrote articles discussing two
main themes: the aspects of Marxism that emphasize the
value of man, and whether there can be alienation under
socialism. The latter included alienation of thought (Maoism had become a virtual religion during the Cultural Revolution, theorists pointed out); political alienation (the revolution was supposed to overcome feudalism but had itself
become a system of feudal control); alienation of power
(high leaders were supposed to serve the people but had

become oppressors of the people); and human alienation (a socialist worker was supposed to be master of his fate but instead was controlled by others). Zhou Yang pointed out that Marx himself said there was no absolute truth, so why should China take Marxism as one? The theorist Su Shaozhi said that if Marxism could not evolve, hard-core leftists would use the old Marxism for their own ends—a "revised" Marxism was necessary as a tool against the Left. General Party Secretary Hu Yaobang spoke of the danger that old ideas could limit people, and the necessity of breaking away from old patterns. Through him, the Central Committee signaled its support of the liberal spirit of the discussions.[7]

Before such ideas were criticized in the autumn, there was a summer ideological campaign against "looking toward money." The economic liberalization had fueled a materialistic trend among people all over the country. Since 1949, they had been told that individual desires must be subsumed to the collective good, that the more they suffered the more "revolutionary" they were. Now for the first time they were allowed to try to live better, and policies had changed to make more comfortable standards possible. Critics claimed that the slogan *xiang qian kan* ("Look toward the future") had become *xiang qian kan* ("Look toward money")—the words for "future" and "money" being Chinese homophones. Backdoorism and corruption were taking place on grander and grander scales. While ordinary people racked their brains over how to get foreign currency to buy low-priced television sets in Guangzhou, high party leaders were finding ways to send their children abroad (despite regulations forbidding such practices) and to get gifts of private automobiles as conditions for signing contracts with foreign firms. The crackdown on economic crimes that took place in late spring and early summer, which resulted in the execution of several high party leaders, was soon felt in the art world, with the criticism of the materialistic trend said to have been exacerbated by the contract system. A June 11 meeting of the Chinese Dramatists' Association emphasized the question of how to establish a "socialist spiritual civilization" and oppose "looking toward money."[8] Some speakers complained that the reforms had been intended to help the arts diversify, not make them into commercial enterprises. Conservatives said that the reforms had contributed to degeneration in the arts (*yishu de duoluo*).

An intensification of the force of the cooler wind came with the publication of the *Works* of Deng Xiaoping. His statements that there was no contradiction between the movement to liberate thought and the Four Basic Principles, and that literature and art should serve socialism, were used to criticize "looking toward money." If the arts were serving business, then they were not in line with party policies. The unhealthy tendencies were creating capitalist civilization, not socialist civilization. Party leadership of the arts was not strong enough. It should be reasserted to help writers and artists struggle against bourgeois ideas.

Writers and artists began to study the *Works*. A meeting of the Chinese Writers' Association discussed the question of consistency with the party, including the importance of criticism/self-criticism and upholding the Four Basic Principles.[9] The Ministry of Culture issued documents calling for a strengthening of arts propaganda work. The Shaanxi Party Committee's propaganda department held a ten-day study class. The local propaganda department established a "Literature and Art Creation Research Group" to investigate and direct the criticism of literature and art; political cadres were called upon to examine performances and visit editorial boards, reporting on what they found.[10]

On August 16 the powerful old party leader Chen Yun

wrote an open letter which was transmitted in document form to the arts units;[11] it became a weapon against the contract system and for greater party control of the arts. Although it concerned the story-telling *pingtan* folk tradition native to the Suzhou region, it was intended to apply to the entire country, just as Chairman Mao had once liked to discuss Hunan's local flower and drum opera because he was especially fond of it, as a way to comment on the general situation in the arts. Here is a sample of Chen's letter:

In recent years, some artists, in the process of our party's implementation of its literature and art policies, have exhibited a divergent tendency. This appears mainly in content and in performance, in an effort to satisfy the low tastes of a part of the audience, and to go after the monetary value of ticket sales. Recently, although the work of managing performances has been strengthened, the problem has not been thoroughly resolved. Now, there are many units which give performances. Aside from the state cultural units, there are workers' associations, neighborhoods, teahouses, stores, even country communes and some individual performers. The managing organizations are responsible only for giving them performing licenses, while the business and financial organizations are responsible only for taxing them. None of them are concerned with the content of the performances. In this situation, it is difficult to rely on the cultural organs to correct the problem of wrong contents and unhealthy performances. It is necessary for the Jiangsu, Zhejiang, and Shanghai Municipal Committees to become involved. All the groups can be called together for a meeting to establish the regulations for managing theaters, determine what kinds of contents should not be permitted and determine what is to be done if they are performed. Then people should be sent to examine the performances, and if they discover violators, deal with them according to the rules. I believe that if control is exerted in this way for several years, the evil wind can be stopped.

Although the contract system for performing artists came to a halt in many provinces in July, Chen Yun's letter sounded its death knell. In September the State Council formally ended it, approving a report from the Ministry of Culture entitled, "Report Concerning Strictly Forbidding Private Individuals from Organizing Performers to Hold Profit-Making Performances."[12] It criticized the unhealthy phenomena of the spring, saying they were a bad influence on the social morals and the thought of young people. Performances once again had to have the approval of performers' units and the local party cultural management. Professional troupes that received invitations to perform had to "give healthy programs, perform earnestly, with modest attitudes. The style should be decent and upright, the life style should be simple, and the money earned should be dealt with according to regulations." Troupes returned to an earlier system of putting on a fixed number of performances a year, as determined by the local cultural organizations. For some artists, it was the end to the largest income they had ever dreamed of; for others, it was a welcome return to normalcy.

In the early 1980s, Chinese writers and artists generally belonged to work units as did other salaried urban Chinese. (There were no arts professionals among the peasantry—if people earned salaries they were by definition no longer peasants.) Performing artists, choreographers, composers, and dramatists belonged to their dance, music, drama, opera, acrobatic, and other troupes; film actors and screen writers to film studios; painters to museums or art schools; and novelists, poets, and short-story writers often to literary magazines, where they held editorial positions. The units issued wages, assigned housing, controlled transfers, held political study meetings, and so on, just as they did for other city dwellers. Units connected with the arts were part of the system controlled at the top by the Ministry of Culture (some publishing houses were under the Ministry of Propaganda). Some, generally those located in Beijing, fell under the direct leadership of the ministry, such as the Central Ballet Troupe, the Central Symphony, the Central Film Studio, the Central Arts Institute, the Art Research Institute, and a number of others. Others, such as the Hunan Drama Troupe or the Shaanxi Film Studio, were controlled by province-level culture departments (*wenhua ting*) or by district, county, or municipal culture bureaus (*wenhua ju*), depending on their rankings. Below these bureaus were small "culture stations" (*wenhua zhan*) in the countryside which were often bases for amateur "propaganda teams" (*xuanchuan dui*) that could be called upon to give performances for national festivals such as Spring Festival, the Party's Birthday, and National Day, and to publicize such party policies as family planning or the Five Stresses, Four Beauties, Three Ardent Loves campaign. Other amateur groups and individual performers were essentially unsupervised, especially in remote areas of the countryside. Urban units such as schools, universities, and factories often also had amateur performing groups, as well as amateur artists in charge of propaganda display cases and "blackboard newspapers" for local news such as the selection of model workers and "Three Good" students.

In addition to belonging to their own units, writers and artists usually belonged to professional associations, at the municipal, provincial, and/or central levels. (The more official recognition they had, the higher their memberships go.) These included: the Chinese Writers' Association, the Chinese Dramatists' Association, the Chinese Musicians' Association, the Chinese Artists' Association, the Chinese Film Workers' Association, the Chinese Dancers' Association, the

Chinese Balladeers' Association, the Chinese Folk Literature and Art Association, the Chinese Photographers' Association, and the Chinese Acrobats' Association.[13]

The associations held meetings during which the party leaders of the associations transmitted documents to the members and conducted conferences and discussions. They published professional magazines or newsletters (among the influential magazines run by the Writers' Association were *People's Literature* (*Renmin Wenxue*), *Nationalities Literature* (*Minzu Wenxue*), *Poetry* (*Shikan*), and *Literature and Art Bulletin* (*Wenyi Bao*). The associations hosted foreign writers and artists. They issued the salaries of a small number of established older writers and artists, becoming, in effect, their work units, although the offices of the associations were generally small and such writers and artists usually worked at home. They also had great influence over a writer's or artist's prestige. Prizes, particularly the national literature and film prizes which were awarded annually beginning in 1978, were highly coveted; regional prizes, such as the Sichuan Province prize in poetry, were also great incentives. No matter what the popularity of a work, however, it rarely gained official recognition if it did not reflect the current party "spirit." (The June 1983 issue of *Literature and Art Bulletin* stated, for example, in an article on prizes: "We cannot say we have no definite standards . . . the Four Basic Principles are our standards. We praise literature that serves the people and serves socialism. We must uphold and develop the tradition of revolutionary literature."[14]) Usually an association could determine whether or not an artist or writer might accept an invitation to go abroad. The screenwriter Bai Hua, for example, was not permitted to go to the U.S. for a conference on modern Chinese literature held at St. John's University in May 1982, whereas Wang Meng, known for toeing the party line despite his experiments with stream-of-consciousness techniques, got his passport. (Wang was also one of two "guests of honor" at the International PEN Congress held in New York in January 1986.)

An association's membership usually spanned many work units and could thus include, in dance for example, performers, teachers, researchers, and choreographers from troupes, schools, and research institutions, while excluding members of these units who were not directly concerned with dance (such as musicians, who had their own association). The various associations fell under the general direction of the China Federation of Literary and Art Circles (*Zhongguo Wenxue Yishujia Lianhe Weiyuanhui*, or *Wenlian*). *Wenlian* had central and provincial branches led by party officials and came under the jurisdiction of the Ministry of Culture. A playwright's unit might thus be a provincial drama troupe, but he might also be a member of his provincial Dramatists' Association, and perhaps, if he was well known, a member of the Chinese Dramatists' Association too. He might then also be a member of the Chinese Writers' and Artists' Association.

The centralized administration of both the work units and the associations, which fanned downward from Beijing into every province and outlying area, was typical of the way China's bureaucracy was organized in all spheres. It made control of lower levels by upper ones comparatively direct, with a clear chain of command at each level. Control over an individual writer or artist was ultimately located at the top level itself—it is no wonder that a remarkable unity was achieved throughout China in the arts, and that it was difficult for anyone to deviate far from the requirements laid down in Beijing.

In many respects, the professional associations supplemented the work units' controls on writers and artists. Their meetings, although far less frequent, were similar to political study meetings; they included document readings, discussions, and sometimes mandatory expressions of attitude. They differed in that they were geared specifically to the art form practiced by the membership. In fact, if the Central Committee wished to criticize a writer, an artist, or specific work, it often did so through such associations. In rarer cases, it became directly involved, arranging for an important party leader to speak to the group to underline the importance the top level attached to what was being said.

Speeches by high leaders at professional meetings often conveyed a new "spirit" which was to guide artistic production until further notice. Deng Xiaoping's speech at the Fourth Congress of Writers and Artists on October 30, 1979, for example, given during a "warm" period, was understood as a signal for experimentation and diversification of subjects and forms. General Party Secretary Hu Yaobang's speech at the Conference on Playwriting in early 1980 blew a cold wind, emphasizing that writers should be more concerned with the social effects of their writing, and specifically criticizing certain works.[15]

An even greater form of control over writers and artists than such speeches and meetings was the mechanisms of approval of an artistic conception. These were different for the various art forms. Control was usually greatest over the spectator arts of film, drama, dance, and opera, for these had the largest audiences, while more flexibility was permitted in literature, which had the smallest. Musicians often encountered attempted control of performance styles, lyrics, and rhythms, with imitations of Hong Kong and Taiwan singers most subject to shifting political winds. With the advent of the general use of large tape recorders, however, regulation became more difficult.

In the early 1980s, there were film companies in Beijing, Shanghai, and Guangzhou, as well as in a small number of provincial capitals. Before 1985 decentralizations gave more autonomy to local studios, a script had to undergo many levels of approval, with emphasis on the film's "message," always the first consideration. The script went to the party leaders of the film unit, to the provincial department of culture, and also to the party leaders in the propaganda bureau in the provincial party committee (or directly to the leaders of the Ministry of Culture and the Ministry of Propaganda if the script was from a central-level company). After the film was shot, it had to be reviewed all over again. Even after completion, it could be withheld without hope of revision, as was Bai Hua's *Unrequited Love* in 1981, if it fell afoul of the party spirit. It could even be withdrawn after it had been released and shown in theaters, as *When People Reach Middle Age* was in late 1983, during the campaign against spiritual pollution, when the film was suddenly considered too humanistic, despite the fact that it was very popular and had been awarded the Golden Rooster Award as one of the best films of 1982.

In drama, dance, and opera, too, the conception had to be approved before work could begin. Every scene, every character, every movement had to be described and passed before other contributors such as composers or set designers could become involved, and certainly before rehearsals could start. Artists involved in the stage arts and film often worked with the knowledge that their project might suddenly be halted at any step of the way, often after months of labor, rehearsals, and even preliminary performances. The negative influence of this on originality was, of course, enormous. Only the most careful saw their work performed with any regularity.

Literature, of all the arts, enjoyed the greatest freedom, not least because censorship was by magazine and book editors rather than by top party ideologists, many of whom had neither the time nor the education to wade through the huge volume of literary material published each month. The various publications thus had considerable autonomy, and if one of them became temporarily "tight," writers were often able to publish their manuscripts somewhere else where things were "looser." Still, the fact that editors had to take responsibility for what they printed was an important constraint. If a piece is selected for public criticism as a warning to others, the editor as well as the writer could often be in serious trouble—he might even lose his position. Despite such risks, it was often possible to find interesting work in local publications even when the top-level publications were railing against obscurantism, bourgeois liberalism, and abstract humanism, as they did during the last quarter of 1983. One way editors protected themselves was by placing a very correct political article in a prominent place at the front of the magazine before proceeding to more controversial work.

The discussion of the necessity for writers and artists to "be consistent" with the Central Committee and serve the people and socialism rather than profit persisted into the autumn of 1983. But it was toward the end of the anticrime campaign that began in August and continued to October that writers and artists were more seriously taken to task. The main targets of the campaign were murderers, rapists, and thieves, and it was welcomed by large sectors of the population who had been afraid of gangs and crimes. But the newspapers seemed to suggest that writers and artists were at least partially responsible for the increase in crime, by spreading doubts about socialism through their works and confusing the "thought" of young people. The increase in disaffection and criminal behavior of the youth thus became the excuse for a major attack on "pollution" in literature and the arts, despite the fact that these things had much more to do with young people's Cultural Revolution upbringing, their rising material expectations, the tantalizing example of the West, and the fact that many of them were unemployed—"waiting for work."

The campaign was set off by such a small event that it seems to have been almost accidental. There was little sign at first that it would affect the art world. On October 11 the Second Plenary Session of the 12th Party Committee passed its "Decision on the Consolidation of the Party." The party rectification of hard-core leftists was to start in 1984 and last for three years, and begin at the top level and work downward to the grass-roots units. Its main targets were to be on the Left, "persons who rose to prominence by following the counterrevolutionary cliques of Lin Biao and Jiang Qing [Mao's wife] in 'rebellion,' those who are seriously factionalist in their ideas, and those who indulged in beating, smashing, and looting." In addition, however, the Decision identified a second "erroneous tendency in the party":

. . . some party members and cadres, who have failed to stand the test of historical setbacks and succumbed to the corrosive influence of bourgeois ideology, doubt and negate the Four Basic Principles, deviate from the party line, principles, and basic policies adopted since the Third Plenary Session of the 11th Party Committee, and propagate bourgeois liberalism. Both these erroneous "Left" and Right tendencies are incompatible with the character and programme and historical mission of the party.[16]

During the meeting, Deng Xiaoping and Chen Yun also gave talks on the problems on the ideological front. Although these talks have not been officially published *in toto*, their general spirit was quickly seized upon by other, conservative party leaders. Armed with the Decision's announcement of the need to crack down on the Right as well as the Left, and with Deng's and Chen's remarks, they launched one of the most dramatic, if also one of the briefest, political movements of contemporary Chinese history.

In fact, the need to combat spiritual pollution had been mentioned in early July, when Chief of Propaganda Deng Liqun spoke to the Party School:

> On the ideological front and on the art front there are many problems, some very serious. A small number of people, including some party members, are carrying the flag of "liberating thought" to oppose Mao Zedong Thought, the socialist system, the leadership of the party, and the people's democratic dictatorship. . . . As for so-called Marxist humanism and socialist alienation, incorrect articles and propaganda have already been a very bad influence. Especially on a portion of young students, the negative influence is very great. All of us comrades involved in propaganda work have a responsibility to use Marxist-Leninist attitudes to analyze earnestly all kinds of wrong thought and industriously wipe out spiritual pollution.[17]

Similar ideas were contained in a report written by Deng Liqun and by Party School Head Wang Zhen to Deng Xiaoping, who then used them during his remarks at the meeting of the Party Committee.[18] Deng Liqun and other conservatives, it seems, pleased at the opportunity that Deng Xiaoping had given them by raising the question on such an important occasion, then proceeded to use the unpublished remarks as ammunition in their own version of struggle against the "Right." Deng Liqun mentioned the Deng Xiaoping speech in a talk published in the October 21 *People's Daily*; the October 23 issue published a speech given by Wang Zhen at the Party School conference, in which he discussed the importance of opposing the Right and spiritual pollution. According to Wang, even in some courses given at the Party School people expounded ideas in opposition to the Four Basic Principles. In the same issue, Peng Zhen, the head of the National People's Congress, tried to give constitutional legitimacy to the suppression of liberalism: "When the constitution says every citizen has the power of free speech, it means such speech cannot violate the Four Basic Principles, it cannot violate the interests of the country and the people." A "Commentary" clarified Peng's words:

As Deng Xiaoping said, we must firmly oppose and overcome the influence of leftist thought. At the same time, we must firmly struggle against thought which doubts the Four Basic Principles. The meaning of spiritual pollution is scattering all kinds of bourgeois and other oppressing classes' rotten and degenerate thought. It is scattering a mood of lacking confidence in socialism, the Communist cause, and the leadership of the party.

Still, none of these statements is very specific about what, exactly, constitutes spiritual pollution, and how to go about eradicating it. On October 31 Minister of Culture Zhu Muzhi explained further:[19]

There are two kinds of spiritual pollution, one, in theory, that violates Marxist principles, and propagates the value of human beings, humanism, and socialist alienation . . . [and a second] within literary and art works, and in performances propagandizing sexual, depraved, terrifying, violent things and the kind of stinking bourgeois life style that consists of looking for fun, drinking, sleeping, and being happy.

It appears that Deng Xiaoping, caught between factions, and also the reformers themselves, as represented by Zhao Ziyang and Hu Yaobang, were not initially opposed to this fanning of a movement. Meanwhile, the major conservative (leftist) elements within the party, including leaders of the Ministry of Propaganda, the Ministry of Culture, and *Red Flag*, the party theoretical journal, may have seen a possible opportunity to oppose the economic reforms and the open door to the West that seemed to them to run so counter to ideological orthodoxy. And other leftist cadres on the middle and lower levels probably thought they could use this as an opportunity to consolidate their power and divert attention from the upcoming party rectification that promised to threaten their power. Soon officials all over the country had taken up the cry, afraid to be caught lagging and later suffer for it.

Most ordinary people not involved in the art world understood the movement as a crackdown on "yellow" practices—pornography, prostitution, and wild sexual parties. And indeed, all over the country, people involved in showing X-rated Hong Kong videotapes were arrested or criticized. These rings were often led by the children of high-ranking party officials (including the son of a vice-governor in Hunan), for they needed foreign connections to get access to such things, and a sense of immunity from constraints that allowed them to do what others dared not. Large numbers of Public Security Bureau personnel were also implicated, for they had stood sentry when tapes were shown and provided protection. In general, ordinary people who had viewed the tapes were simply admonished, but party members were expelled. Those who had made a profit from such activities or who provided facilities for showing tapes were sentenced severely or sent for labor reform.[20] As for other "yellow" transgressions, prostitutes and pimps (who were frequently executed) continued to be arrested as they had beginning earlier in the fall, while "black light dances," wild parties held among students and workers that involved much groping in the dark, were suppressed. Printed materials were also examined, and in at least some cases, nudes by serious Western artists were confiscated along with genuine pornography.

The crackdown on "yellow" tendencies was a comparatively clear-cut task for the party, and it did not worry most of the populace, which had nothing to do with such things. More complex were the questions of "pollution" in theory and literature and art, and the crackdown in those fields did affect the general climate for intellectual freedom. Ultimately, the people's ability to think and speak critically of socialism and the party was under fire. Only part of the party's efforts to solve the crisis of confidence involved dealing with the phenomena which caused it, such as low living standards and party corruption; the other aspect of its efforts involved propaganda and, when that failed, coercion.

The literary and art worlds came under attack as in this example:

In literary creation, some people . . . lack zeal in depicting and singing the praises of the revolutionary history of the party and people and their heroic achievements in the drive for building socialist modernization . . . they are keen on depicting darkness and even randomly distorting revolutionary history and reality. Some people have advocated the trend of the so-called modernist school of the West, have openly preached that the ultimate aim of literature and art is self-expression, and brazenly advertised abstract humanity and humanitarianism . . . some people have attempted to advocate out-and-out egoism, nihilism, and pessimism under the pretext of exploring life. Some people have flagrantly advertised sexual liberation and concocted pornographic stories to harm the readers' souls under the guise of manifesting human nature. Some people have insisted on writing on trivial matters and eternal subjects in an attempt to lead the people to the evil way of having no ideals at all. Some literary periodicals have published on a large scale their special love issues carrying pictures of pretty girls on the cover to attract more readers. . . .[21]

Soon after the cry against spiritual pollution was raised, some of China's veteran writers hastened to participate. Ding Ling was among the first:[22]

If light music is played in the theaters, everyone applauds, but when they hear serious music, no one does. It's even gotten to the point that when someone sings, "Without the Communist Party, There Would be No New China," people laugh derisively. Another peculiar thing is that just because some foreign scholars praise certain works, our people think they are good. Young people like liberalism too much. . . .

The middle-aged writer Wang Meng also spoke about the importance of opposing the rightist tendency and bourgeois liberalism. He even said writers should "earnestly study the works of Chairman Mao," always an indication of an increasingly orthodox climate.[23] Ai Qing, too, the well-respected poet, revived criticisms of obscure poetry and young people's aesthetic theories.[24]

With these well-publicized preparations, and the self-criticism made by the leading proponent of Marxist humanism and socialist alienation, Zhou Yang (of which more later), the China Federation of Literary and Art Circles held a meeting (reported November 10)[25] to discuss the "spirit" of the 12th Party Committee. Speeches were given by the leading cultural officials, including Zhou Yang himself, who acknowledged once again that he had a responsibility for the spread of spiritual pollution and said he welcomed others' further criticisms. Others emphasized the presence of unhealthy tendencies in literature and the arts and the need to oppose the Right as well as the Left. Representatives from the branch artists' associations of most of China were present, and when they returned to their various provinces they were armed not only with Central Committee documents but also with these "mobilizing reports." They too held meetings, eliciting "attitudes" and inducing self-criticism where it was thought necessary.

One outcome of the mobilization in the art world was the closing of certain magazines. In Guangzhou, where leftist influence in the arts was strong, *October (Shiyue)*, *Flower City (Huacheng)*, *Guangzhou Literature and Art (Guang-*

zhou Wenyi), *Zhan River* (*Zhan Jiang*), and *Guangzhou Hygiene* (*Guangzhou Weisheng*) were all named by the Provincial Party Committee for criticism. *Guangzhou Hygiene*, perhaps guilty of publishing articles on sex that were deemed unhealthy, and *Young Explorers* (*Shaonian Tansuozhe*), which must have printed too many humanistic, modernistic stories, were closed down. In Yunnan Province, *Gejiu Literature and Art* (*Gejiu Wenyi*), which had published a story by Yu Luojing, "A Fairy Tale in Spring" (*Chuntian de Tonghua*) about the sexual oppression of women, also had to stop publishing, and Zhejiang Province's *South of the River* (*Jiangnan*) was another victim on account of its polluting stories.[26]

Some magazines experienced a reshuffling of editors rather than an all-out shutdown. Open-minded editors were transferred away or put in less authoritative positions. The editor-in-chief of the influential *Poetry* lost his job, and a new position of "adviser" was filled by the leftist poet Zhang Kejia. *Shanghai Literature* (*Shanghai Wenxue*) got a new editor, while *People's Literature* in Peking had been feeling the cooler wind since August, when Wang Meng came in as the new chief editor. There was also an important shakeup at the *People's Daily*.

Although a number of literary works were attacked, three works received the brunt of the criticism. They express many of the sensitive themes other writers were dealing with. They are: Li Ping's *When Sunset Disappears*, Dai Houying's *People, Ah People*, and Zhang Xiaotian's *Sparse Prairie Grasses*. Although all three had been criticized before, the attacks were renewed with force during the campaign against spiritual pollution.

Li Ping's novel is divided into four parts, Spring, Summer, Winter, and Autumn, and tells the tragic love story of a couple during the ten-year Cultural Revolution.

Spring: The male protagonist, Li Huaiping, is the son of a People's Liberation Army general. The woman, Nan Shuang, is the granddaughter of a Guomindang (KMT) general. The two meet in a park and each secretly falls in love with the other. Although Nan lends Li an edition of Shakespeare, they separate without knowing each others' names.

Summer: The Cultural Revolution has begun, and Li has become a Red Guard leader. He takes his group on a "search raid" of Nan's grandfather's home to look for "reactionary" artifacts. In the course of cross-examining the old man, he discovers that he and Li's father once had great admiration for one another, despite the fact that they were adversaries during the civil war. As Nan witnesses the Red Guards' treatment of her grandfather, her secret love for Li is shaken.

Winter: The fighting is over and "educated youths," or middle-school graduates, are being sent to the countryside to become peasants. Li is seeing off some classmates; the KMT general and his wife are seeing off Nan. Li overhears Nan saying that, after countless humiliations, she has now given her faith to the Christian God. Her grandparents express the wish that she find a husband, and he hears her tell them how she once loved the Red Guard who led the raid on their home.

Autumn: After twelve years, Li has also become a victim of the Cultural Revolution. His mother, imprisoned during factional struggles, has died in prison, and he has lost touch with his father. Li is now an officer in the navy. On leave, he visits the sacred mountain, Taishan, where he meets an old Buddhist monk who makes a deep impression on him. He also encounters a group of foreign tourists, and it turns out that their interpreter is Nan. Li tries to restore the love between them, telling her that both of them are equally scarred by the revolution, but Nan says she has lost all will to love or hate, and wishes only to withdraw from the world.

When Sunset Disappears was very popular among young people, for most had had comparable experiences, and the novel evoked their pasts, their sorrows, and their search for something to believe in. Many had been through the same stages of idealism and disillusionment—indeed, the novel seemed to justify the crisis of confidence. This viewpoint was considered so unacceptable that after the book was published in January 1981,[27] it was criticized in *China Youth Daily, Literature and Art Bulletin*, and *Works and Discussion (Zuopin yu Zhengming)*.[28] Critics said the author showed a lack of historical knowledge, and claimed that the book's conclusion conflicted with the revolutionary emphasis on working to build the motherland.

In late 1983 the novel was attacked again for its humanitarianism, humanism, and religious spirit. It did not depict the characters from the standpoint of class struggle, detractors wrote. How could a KMT general, an enemy of the Chinese people, be shown to weep? This kind of general who had fought against the party and served the KMT should be considered with respect to his class background and political position. The social effects of his behavior had to be evaluated. Another problem was that the novel did not show the outcome of the struggle between Communists and KMT as hatred. If there was no enmity, why then had there been a civil war?

According to the colorful remarks of *People's Literature*'s chief editor Wang Meng, the novel

distorts revolutionary history and revolutionary reality. It betrays the basic principles of Marxism, beautifies the landlord capitalist class, negates class struggle, and negates the necessity of revolutionary struggle. It praises a non-revolutionary humanism which supersedes class and party. This is the farting of idealism, it is the farting of bourgeois humanism in opposition to Marxist class theory.[29]

As for the novel's religious theme, it was said to constitute an attack on Communism. The author implied that religion, not the party, could resolve young people's unhappiness; by supporting religious fervor, he was virtually advocating the crisis of belief.

Dai Houying's *People, Ah, People* was also attacked primarily for its humanitarian themes. It was called "not a good novel because it advocates abstract human nature and bourgeois humanitarianism."[30] One proof of this was supposed to be Dai Houying's own story, which indicated that her background was full of pernicious humanism.[31] It seems that during the Cultural Revolution, as a Red Guard, Dai Houying had been assigned the task of cross-examining a certain counterrevolutionary poet. During their talks, she came to have sympathy for him, and eventually to love him. When she asked Red Guard leaders for permission to marry him, it was denied, and she was thrown out of the organization in punishment. The poet was attacked so vociferously that at last he could stand it no longer and killed himself. Dai failed to find a publisher for her first novel, a remembrance of her lover called *The Death of a Poet*. Later, in *People, Ah, People*, she began to explore humanitarian themes more indirectly. To the consternation of ideologists, her work was so popular that there were four printings within half a year.

In the novel, Dai shows how the leftist political line brings unhappiness to four intellectuals, leaving permanent psychological scars. Her tone is predominantly poetic and philosophical, as reflected in this passage, which was cited for criticism:

People are like stars in the sky. They all have their own places and right to exist. Without relying on anyone to hold them up, they are still in the sky. Without being held up by anyone, you too have the right to live on this earth.

According to critics, the problem with these ideas was that they implied that the party was superfluous, and also that all people had basic rights. (In the orthodox party view, in a class society certain people do not have rights.)

Many of the other criticisms of *People, Ah, People* revolved around alleged distortions of the situation of intellectuals. According to one critic, since the party was now taking good care of intellectuals, Dai Houying's portrait of them as still oppressed and underutilized was "not in accordance with the facts." She was said to exacerbate the conflict between intellectuals and the party, and to show the socialist system as inhumane and therefore responsible for the unhappiness of the people.

Dai Houying resisted pressures to criticize herself. At one point she said:

I'm not afraid to wear the cap [label] of self expression. . . . If a person takes up a pen to write, it is because in his heart he has some special feeling to express. It is fantasy to think that literary creation can be separated from self-expression, or else it shows a lack of understanding of art.[32]

During the campaign against spiritual pollution, Dai never published a self-criticism, despite the fact that she was summoned precipitously back from Guangzhou (where she was in an editorial conference on the publication of a new story) to Shanghai to be criticized by the local department of culture. Foreigners who asked to meet her during the autumn of 1983 were told it was "not convenient." Her postscript to *People, Ah, People* also reveals her to be unusually courageous:

I feel as if I have just awakened from a dream. Although the cold sweat is not yet dry, and my soul is not yet quiet, at least I am awake. I want to proclaim my awakening to people like myself, so this is why I write. . . . I write of the traces of people's blood and tears, of the weeping unhappiness of distorted souls, of the sparks of hearts lighting up in the darkness. I loudly shout, "Soul, come back!" With boundless joy I record the renaissance of humanism.

Chinese often use the term "awakening" (*xing guolai*) to refer to their disillusionment with mass political movements. Dai speaks thus to the generation who turned to human relationships to fill the emptiness that was left when they realized they had been manipulated and deceived during the Cultural Revolution.

The third work highly criticized in late 1983, *Sparse Prairie Grasses*, published in February 1982 in Changchun,[33] is by Zhang Xiaotian. The novella covers the period from 1948 to 1980, and, like *When Sunset Disappears*, it deals with KMT and PLA (People's Liberation Army) officers. In 1948, after a major battle, a KMT general named Sheng escapes and, tired, hungry, and wounded, faints in the snow. He awakens in a bed in a damp sweet potato cellar, his wound having been dressed by a peasant woman named Du. Also staying in Du's home is an eighteen-year-old PLA officer, a woman named Su. When she discovers Sheng, the two have a gun fight. The peasant woman, interceding, is wounded; out of guilt toward the woman who saved his life, Sheng surrenders and is taken to prison.

Twenty years later, in 1968, Sheng is sent back to the same village to be reformed through labor. Meanwhile Su, the PLA officer, has become a party secretary of the district, but with the advent of the Cultural Revolution has been accused of being a capitalist roader. Now she too has been sent to the village for labor reform. An added twist is that the person supervising the laborers is Sheng's daughter, although neither she nor Sheng is aware of the fact. (During the civil war Sheng's wife remarried thinking Sheng dead, and gave her new husband's name to their small daughter.) The daughter, a Red Guard very loyal to Chairman Mao, is soon to be promoted to an important city post. However, during a routine background check, it is discovered who she really was. Unable to bear the truth, she drowns herself.

Meanwhile, the peasant woman Du continues to intercede between Su and Sheng. Her sympathetic attitude angers the leftists, and she is criticized. To save her, Sheng fabricates some diaries portraying himself as a spy who has deliberately tried to make people suspicious of her so as to be rid of her. Du is spared, but Sheng returns to prison.

Many years later, the woman Su's son, a participant in the 1976 Tiananmen Incident, is sought by the Public Security Bureau and escapes to the village. Du shelters him in the cellar and keeps certain incriminating photographs for him. When the photos are found in her possession, she is sent to prison. She is released after the fall of the Gang of Four, near death. The old enemies Su and Sheng go to see her. With her last breath she reveals Sheng's kindness to Su's son while he hid in the cellar. The story concludes in an atmosphere of tragic awareness of wasted lives and unnecessary enmities.

The problem, for critics, with the peasant woman Du was that her humanitarianism is uninfluenced by political considerations or philosophies. At one point she says, "I do not believe in spirits and ghosts. I feel that human beings living on the earth should pity the unfortunate, take care of the old, do what is right by their own hearts. Only if you see others as human beings will they see you as one."

The author's message, that political struggles have twisted normal human relationships, and that love and trust are the true ways to solve social problems, proved anathema to the critics of bourgeois humanism. Another problem was that Zhang's portrayal of the peasant woman "distorted revolutionary history": in accordance with her class background, she should be an ardent PLA supporter, for hadn't the PLA liberated the peasants? Furthermore, Zhang seemed to be attributing a strange power to humanism. In battle, the KMT general remained adamant, but in the face of the peasant woman's kindness he surrendered like a sheep. This was unrealistic. He should, of course, have yielded before the superior strength of the PLA.

The work was also said to have a peculiar vision of the moral development of the characters. Although Sheng was sentenced to labor reform, the change in his attitude came not because of the success of the party's political thought education work, but because of internal reflection. According to Zhang's portrayal, the party's work seemed ineffectual. Finally, the author was guilty of ignoring the political victories of the party over the Gang of Four. He had forgotten that the party had already "summed up the lessons of history" and corrected the wrong leftist line. On his own, he was using bourgeois humanism to describe the disorders of the Cultural Revolution, drawing from it the lesson that human feeling without regard to class background was the solution to China's ills. This was incorrect. The lesson of the Cultural Revolution was to guard against leftist excesses, but not to invalidate the party.[34]

In a 1982 letter to a friend, Zhang had said he knew he was taking a risk in publishing the novel, but felt it was worth it:

Humanism, humanitarianism, the value of human beings—these have all been questions which have made people as frightened as if they had seen a tiger. But as I have said, if you do not confront these questions, they will confront you, so this time, I went ahead and took the risk. . . . After the ten-year period of disorder, what kind of humanism is left? Then one could casually insult people's characters, put on labels, struggle against them, paint their faces black, cut the vocal cords of those sentenced to death . . . these are terrifying, inhumane things. Was this not a reactionary time in human history? To expose these ugly things, to propagandize humanism, should not be in contradiction with socialism.[35]

On December 19, 1983, Zhang sang a very different tune in an essay called "Never Forget the Responsibility of Socialist Writers," hailed as the fruit of his reeducation by the Jilin Provincial Party Committee and the Changchun Film Studio.[36]

As a writer who is also a party member, I feel very guilty and sad to write on this subject. I now feel deeply that in writing *Sparse Prairie Grasses*, a story with serious mistakes in thought and art, I did not fulfill my responsibility as a socialist writer, and did not live up to the honor of being a party member. . . . What I propagandized in this story superseded class humanitarian views, violated Marxist class theory, and showed a liberal tendency. . . . It showed an incorrect understanding and evaluation of life. The basic reason is that I ignored the guidance of Marxism–Leninism–Mao Zedong Thought in the practice of literature. . . .

Many young people had written to Zhang saying that they had learned from the peasant woman Du how to be human beings, and that the novel was enjoying tremendous popularity in the colleges. Citing such responses as evidence of the negative impact of his work, Zhang managed, even while criticizing himself, to defend it. Readers who had enjoyed his novel would have understood that Zhang had been pressured into writing a self-criticism, and would not have thought any the worse of him for it.

Science fiction came under attack during the campaign against spiritual pollution because, according to a report on a meeting of the Science and Technology Commission, some writers were writing about ghosts and sex in the name of science fiction, and others were using science fiction to express dissatisfaction with socialism.[37]

Utopianism in some science fiction did indeed often imply criticism of the status quo. According to a *Los Angeles Times* article by Michael Parks, for example, the nine space travelers in Meng Weizai's *Interview with Missing Persons* tell of a planet "where they found an ideal society in which everyone is equal, eternally youthful and full of pure love, where the leader-president is not first but last, where all seek wisdom and where evil is so unknown that there are not even words in the dictionary for it."[38]

In an interview, leading science fiction writer and astronomer Zheng Wenguang is quoted as saying:

> In outer space, there is no capitalism, no socialism and no political problems to worry us. . . . The inner workings of man are more interesting than space travel . . . by using such science fiction, I can make people see the period and its problems more profoundly. It is not only past problems I want to examine, but the roots of the tragedies (such as the Cultural Revolution) within ourselves.[39]

Thus through the genre of science fiction, many writers hoped to escape the careful surveillance that was the norm for other forms of writing. Science fiction, by definition, involved fantasy, other realities, and fabulous possibilities. Furthermore, since, according to Marxist theory, pure science could be considered apolitical, science fiction writers had a ready-made excuse for working comparatively independently.

However, during the anti–spiritual pollution campaign science fiction was not exempt. A November 5, 1983, article summed up the problems with it: There was too much violence, and the violence was too often linked to science and technology. The presence of supermen with godlike powers implied that ordinary human beings were not fully capable of controlling their society. Some stories did not really describe science but rather the writers' opposition to the party: they were faithful neither to science, to life, nor to Communist ideals. Many were said to use the fact that they were writing about science as a cloak to escape ordinary criticism—this was why more and more science fiction stories had been written in recent years. Such stories were especially dangerous because so much of the readership was young children. (What were they to think, the author of the article demanded, when the aliens from another planet got off their spaceships and criticized the socialist system?)[10]

On December 22 the editorial board of *Literature and Art Bulletin* and the China Federation of Literary and Art Circles' Theory Research Office held a meeting on science fiction writing, chaired by the now-chastened Zhou Yang.[41] Once again it was pointed out that some writers used robots and aliens from outer space to show their doubts about party leaders and to describe life styles superior to those in the socialist world. Science fiction was seen as almost as bad an influence as pornography on the thought of young people, both sharing a responsibility for the recent upsurge in social disorder. This meeting was held after much of the campaign had quieted down, indicating prospects for greater surveillance of the content of science fiction, and for the future sway of the Four Basic Principles even on other planets.

The so-called "obscure" school of poetry had, at one point, moved from unofficial publications into a temporary place in the mainstream. Shu Ting's work, for example, first published in the underground *Today*, then in the regional *Star* (*Xingxing*) in Sichuan (where the senior editor was the open-minded ex-rightist poet Liu Shahe), appeared in the influential *Poetry* in April and November 1980. Her work, and other work like it, had found supporters among liberal editors and party theorists and among a new breed of young literary theoreticians whose work was exemplified by three articles called the "Three Rising Ups": "Before the New Uprising" (*Zai Xin de Jueqi Mianqian*), written by an established editor and published in May 1980[42] "New Aesthetic Principles Are Rising Up" (*Xin de Meixue Yuanze Zai Jueqi*), written by a student from Fujian Teachers' College and published in March 1981[43] and "Group of Rising-up Poems" (*Jueqi de Shiqun*) written by Xu Jingya, a student at Jilin University and published in January 1983.[44]

It was the latter article that generated the most controversy during the campaign against spiritual pollution for the essay came out very late, well after the 1981 movement to criticize obscure poetry, and therefore seemed a blatant defiance of the current of the times.

Xu Jingya was a thirty-three-year-old Chinese literature student and a modernist poet in his own right. He managed to get his graduation thesis published in Lanzhou's *Contemporary Literature and Art Thought* (*Dangdai Wenyi Sichao*), in an example of the relative independence of the mood at the top often found in local literary circles. The thesis defined "new poetry" as reflecting the ideals, thoughtfulness, and troubles of China's youth, their anxiety for the future, and their determination not to be tricked again by political manipulators. He described modern poets as believing in the power and will of man, and as seeing themselves first and foremost as human beings with a capacity for self-expression. Poetry was called "the history of the soul of the poet . . . what the poet creates is his own world."

This article expressed so many views abhorrent to party arts officials that, according to a November 3, 1983, report, a meeting of more than sixty theorists was held especially to criticize it.[45] Xu's thesis not only opposed socialist aesthetics, they said, but it also expressed political views that clearly violated socialist theory. Especially serious was that the party had called for correction of liberal tendencies before the publication of the article, but Xu had proceeded to write and publish it anyway. Xu was present at the meeting, and he made the requisite self-criticism.

Many other meetings and articles criticized modernism in poetry and the Three Rising Ups.[46] In Chongqing, for example, more than thirty poets and critics attended a meeting on the theme "Discussing Poetry." Because theory on art had been inconsistent with the socialist road, speakers said, poetry had been brought to a state of disorder.[47] Others criticized the Three Rising Ups for encouraging poets to express themselves rather than mirror reality: the authors were accused of negating the socialist poetic tradition, and of being influenced by Western modernism. Some noted a discrepancy between the older and younger generations.[48] Even the army began to criticize poetry: *PLA Literature and Art* (*Jiefang Jun Wenyi*) and *PLA Daily* (*Jiefang Jun Bao*) called a meeting in October 1983 to denounce the pollution of poetry and its readers by bourgeois liberalism.[49]

In general, the theory tended to be blamed for the poetry, although in fact the poetry had appeared and become popular before theorists spoke out to justify it artistically. Few individual poems were criticized during 1983, but one, a long poem by Yang Lian called *Ruorelang* which appeared in May, was attacked for its obscure experiments with Tibetan religious themes.[50] Two other, earlier poems were also mentioned: "Answer" (*Huida*) by Bei Dao, which proclaimed, "I tell you, world, I don't believe!"[51] and "Assembly Line" (*Liu Shui Xian*) by Shu Ting, which showed mechanization as a tool for turning people into slaves ("But strange—the only thing I cannot feel is my own existence").[52] According to the critics, people should not respond to darkness with disbelief but with optimism and determination; in a cold winter, they should use a torch to warm themselves.

Most experiments with modernism in poetry had ceased after the criticisms of late 1981; Xu Jingya's audacity in reviving a sensitive debate may have been responsible for the new wave of criticism that occurred during the final months of 1983. But the criticisms were also a reflection of the persistent popularity of such works. Indeed, criticisms in China, as in other countries, have often had the unwanted effect of drawing even greater attention to the works. It is often assumed that anything the party does not like must be very interesting. The refusal of obscure poetry to die out may also be traced, in part, to a practical factor: poetry is easier to copy and pass about than longer works.

In addition to the self-appointed theorists of new poetry, more established "theorists" were attacked in the autumn of 1983. "Theorists" generally included party ideologists and literature and art theorists, among them teachers at the Central Party School and its branches; researchers at such branches of the Academy of Social Sciences as the History Research Institute and Philosophy Research Institute; the many teachers of political theory and aesthetics in China's universities, academies, and middle schools; and certain columnists and writers for newspapers and magazines. Representatives of these groups were present at the important Conference on Mao Zedong's Literary and Art Thought held under the direction of the China Federation of Literary and Art Circles from October 5 to 11, 1983, in Shandong Province. The meeting was an early sign of tightening in the theory world. More than twenty leading theorists spoke, emphasizing the need to uphold a socialist direction for literature and art, to study the works of Chairman Mao, and to oppose self-expression and liberalism.[53]

Another early sign of constraint was an October 8 *Guangming Daily* article, "On the Ideological Front, the Marxist-Leninist Standpoint Must Be Upheld." It warned members of the scholarly and theoretical world that there were dangers in their "thought." Under conditions of openness to the outside world, bourgeois influence could easily slip in; some critics and theorists had been overeager to introduce Western ideas and ended up spreading bourgeois liberalism; some scholars had translated and published Western scholarly and literary works but had not appied Marxist-Leninist criticism to them, so young people were negatively influenced. The works of Sartre, for example, had been introduced indiscriminately, and now many young people were adopting existentialism. This was considered partially the fault of the theorists.

It is not surprising that the world of theory began to tighten up before the campaign against spiritual pollution was fully launched. Deng Liqun, as propaganda chief, and Wang Zhen, as head of the Party School, had great power over theorists, and they, of course, were largely responsible for the drive against spiritual pollution. After Deng Xiaoping gave apparent official blessing to that campaign in mid-October, the theory front became even more active. During a meeting held from November 5 to 8, 1983, in Beijing, attended by more than a hundred theorists, Deng Liqun blamed the disorder among party theorists for the disorder in the thought of the young.[54] A "National Mao Zedong Thought Discussion Meeting" on November 12 in Guangxi Province brought more than five hundred participants from twenty-eight provinces. Many famous party history teachers, scholars, and theorists were present.[55] On November 26 *Red Flag*, the party theoretical journal, invited twenty-odd writers and artists for a discussion rejecting the notion of socialist alienation.

Those criticized had to acknowledge their mistakes publicly. On November 1 Xing Fensi, the distinguished head of the Philosophy Research Institute of the Academy of Social Sciences and a proponent of theories of Marxist humanism and socialist alienation, was interviewed by reporters. He stated that spiritual pollution had become a serious problem, not only in theory and in literature and art, but also in journalism, education, and law. Each field influenced the other and so the pollution spread. It ran deep, he said. Even now, many people were dragging their feet, unwilling to speak out and write against it.[56]

At the center of the controversy in the theory field was the veteran party and cultural official Zhou Yang, chairman of the China Federation of Literary and Art Circles. He had been an outspoken proponent of liberal ideas, yet now he was expected to lead the campaign against spiritual pollution in literature and the arts. Therefore his "mistakes" had to be dealt with directly and visibly, in order to clear the way for the movement. His self-criticism was published in an interview in the November 5 *People's Daily*.

Zhou Yang said that he supported the decision to rectify the party and eliminate spiritual pollution, and he criticized his own articles on socialist alienation and Marxist humanism. In publishing these articles, he acknowledged, he had not been careful. Such matters were very complicated. He had been incorrect to discuss them at such an inappropriate time as the important occasion of the 100th anniversary of the death of Karl Marx, where, given his own high position, his remarks were certain to elicit wide attention. Furthermore, when others had criticized his views, he had wrongfully maintained his position and argued with them, rather than mending his ways. He confessed responsibility for the disorder in the world of theory and for shaking the confidence of the people in the socialist cause. He had not fulfilled his responsibility to the party. Finally he is said to have sighed, "To be a real Marxist, to be a thorough materialist, this is not an easy thing."

The party then launched an all-out attack on Zhou's ideas: one should not view certain problems of the socialist system as socialist alienation; one should not emphasize "abstract humanism," since the only true humanism was socialist humanism, whereby people serve the society and the society serves the people. Discussions such as Zhou's caused people to mistrust the socialist system. If people believed that socialist alienation was possible, they would eventually turn against the leadership of the party.[57]

Also criticized were Western Marxists who emphasized the humanism in the works of the young Marx, including the New Marxists of the Frankfurt School, and the American philosopher Sidney Hook.[58] The work of C. T. Hsia, a professor at Columbia University, was attacked, for Hsia admired certain writers whom the party ignored, such as Shen Congwen, while he deprecated such party models as Lu Xun, Guo Moruo, and Ding Ling.[59]

According to movement activists, spiritual pollution could not be eliminated quickly but required long-term vigilance. The open discussion in ideology and in literary and art theory that had been possible for part of the post-Mao period thus came to a halt. The implications, beyond the arts, for social sciences and for academic freedom in general were clear. If discussion of such questions as the emergence of a new privileged class, of the anomie of the workers, and of the deification of Mao were impossible, then there could be no intellectually honest discussion of problems facing China. And if Marx's humanistic aspects could not be integrated into official ideology, the crisis of confidence would remain unresolved: people would continue to believe in their hearts that the negation of basic humanitarian values lay at the heart of the mutual betrayals that led, during the Cultural Revolution, to national tragedy.

The spectator arts of dance, drama, and film got through the campaign against spiritual pollution relatively easily, primarily because the system of approval already in force tended to veto problematic works long before they reached potential viewers. The dance world was primarily concerned with such questions as how to re-choreograph folk and minority dances so as to make them suitable for performance and yet retain their authenticity; how to preserve original materials before old artists died, and what notation systems to use; and how to create a Chinese dance style (the ballet brought in during the fifties with the Soviet presence had become dominant during the Cultural Revolution, when folk styles were considered politically suspect). After the success of *The Silk Route* (choreographed by the Gansu Song and Dance Troupe), a number of other dance-dramas were created drawing on China's historical traditions. The Hubei Song and Dance Troupe's *Chime Bells Music and Dance*, for example, was based on fifth-century-B.C. instruments and murals. For many of the most important dance troupes, the end of 1983 marked the climax of the production of *Song of the Revolution*, a massive dance-drama on the history of the Chinese Communist party, in which more than a thousand dancers and choreographers from seventeen units participated. The film of the performance was released in 1984. The contents, which glossed over the Cultural Revolution years, were carefully checked by party leaders before the shooting.[60]

In drama, also, the exploration of historical themes was an apparently safer and subtler way to express one's views. Bai Hua's drama *Emperor Wu's Golden Lance and Emperor Yue's Sword* (*Wuwang Jinge, Yuewang Jian*) was performed in February. Foreign plays were welcome as long as they criticized capitalism: Arthur Miller's *Death of a Salesman* appeared in Beijing in the spring of 1983, with Miller himself, at the invitation of the Chinese Dramatists' Association, directing. A play by Sartre, however, was closed in Shanghai, and a Chinese play by Gao Xingjian, *Bus Stop* (*Chezhan*), said to be influenced by existentialism, was closed in Beijing. *Bus Stop* describes people waiting for ten years at a bus stop for a bus that never arrives, implying that many years after their socialist revolution, the Chinese people are still waiting for their problems to be solved. Even after the campaign against spiritual pollution was over, the play continued to be criticized, as in an article in the March 1984 *Literature and Art Bulletin*.

If the official performing-arts units escaped the campaign with little more trouble than reminders of the dangers of "looking toward money," for amateur groups it was another story. These groups had not been subject to party inspection and supervision, and, in the countryside, many folk traditions and beliefs had persisted as they had not among educated city dwellers. Moreover, the peasants, under the responsibility system, now had money to pay for performances, and these flourished. But they were not so popular with official monitors. A November 1, 1983, Henan Province radio broadcast accused amateurs as follows:[61]

On the theatrical stage, a number of literary and art organizations . . . have vigorously performed programs describing indiscriminate loyalty and filial piety, retribution of sin, and feudal superstition to meet the low taste of some audiences. Some of the so-called amateur theatrical troupes and old artists have gone around performing pornographic and terror plays.

"Indiscriminate loyalty and filial piety," we may surmise, like abstract humanism and humanitarianism, were seen as competing with people's sense of duty to the party and the state.

"Pornographic and terror plays" apparently referred to seductive costuming and gestures, and to ghost stories.

An October 30, 1983, report on the situation in Anhui Province[62] related how a number of old performances from feudal society had been revived. The article complained that some units had not taken a firm stance against unauthorized shows. (Old local folk artists, who had been professionals before Liberation, were doubtless performing again in Anhui, as they were in many rural areas using oral traditions that had never undergone party approval.) Many performances were said to be of low level, conveying no socialist values. Some of the performers even had "complicated backgrounds" (i.e., were out of work, had been imprisoned, or had "bad" class origins). The Anhui Culture Department called on the culture bureaus of each district, city, and county to investigate such performers by checking on their backgrounds and their residence permits. Only those licensed by these organizations were to have the right to perform, but they could not take their shows from one area to another without special permission. Each area's culture bureau was to hold strict examinations of programs, eliminating any that showed "unhealthy" tendencies. Finally, party secretaries were to monitor the development of the "political thought" of amateur performers, holding special political study classes for them twice a year. All this work was to be assisted by the local Public Security Bureau personnel, who would keep tabs on performers' activities and ensure that no deviation from these rules occurred.

Film, once the art form most stridently denounced, had by late 1983 become one of the most conservative. After the 1981 attacks on *Unrequited Love*, filmmakers had been taught yet another lesson: Shen Rong's *When People Reach Middle Age*, which had received all kinds of honors, was attacked in June 1983 for exaggerating the difficulties of intellectuals and for portraying two "traitors," characters who decide to leave China for the United States.[63] If such a highly recognized, carefully chosen script could be criticized, it was not surprising that by the time the campaign against spiritual pollution came along little remained in the movies for leftists to complain about.

In the music world, the primary issue during the campaign against spiritual pollution was "light music." Popular music from Hong Kong and Taiwan, especially that of the Taiwan singer Deng Lijun, had become increasingly widespread since the opening of the door to the West.[64] More and more people were able to afford large tape recorders, and it became fashionable for young people to carry them around in parks and to hold dance parties in their homes. The lyrics of "light music," often sentimental and individualistic, were called "bourgeois drugs" that weakened young people's revolutionary energy. The singing styles, soft and sexy, were seen as dangerous pollution. Yet the well-distributed bootleg tapes, both those smuggled in and those illegally manufactured within China, were clearly not going to be eliminated overnight. As the joke went, China was "governed by the two Dengs: during the day people listened to Deng Xiaoping, at night, to Deng Lijun."

An October 1983 article in *People's Music (Renmin Yinyue)*[65] chastised manufacturers of records and tapes for forgetting to "consider the social effects" of light music. Performers were said to be guilty of using foreign instruments such as electric guitars and drums, and when they played they swayed their bodies, while flickering red lights "made people's heads spin, making them wonder if they had come to a Hong Kong bar." It was said to be difficult to tell whether a singer was from China, Hong Kong, or Taiwan—all the songs were about love, butterflies, flowers, birds, moonlight, friendship, and seashores. This frivolity, *People's Music* complained, affected the revolutionary ardor of the people.

In the same issue, an article criticized a fifteen-year-old singer named Cheng Lin who had become popular through a film appearance.[66] The Beijing Tape Recorder Factory had violated government rules and recorded a tape of eighteen of her songs, illegally selling 30,000 copies. The article complained that even when Cheng sang revolutionary songs they sounded as if they came from Hong Kong. Her parents, it was suggested, should teach her to avoid the corrupt road of the Taiwan singing stars.

Another article, "What Kind of Light Music Do We Need?" described the situation as that of the "Five Manys": many performances, listeners, profits, problems, and discussions. The author, an official in the Musicians' Association, complained of depravity and of singers who deceived inspectors:

Some units, in order to increase their incomes, satisfy low tastes. Female singers, and even some male ones, wiggle their hips as they sing, and their performance costumes are more and more revealing, transparent, and strange! Even more serious is that they prepare two programs and two performance styles. When leaders come to inspect, they show one set; when they sell tickets and perform, they show another. This is highly irregular . . . these performers should be given an education in Marxist aesthetics, to teach them what kind of beauty is needed in contemporary China.

During the height of the campaign against spiritual pollution, young people were ordered to turn in their tapes, and in some cases to have them re-recorded with revolutionary music. The Zhejiang Song and Dance Troupe was organized into singing teams to give free concerts in neighborhoods, factories, and middle schools in Hangzhou as a means of combatting pollution.[67]

The Press

By 1983, many Chinese felt they had more access to information than at any time in their recent history. Their newspapers might fail to report earthquakes, floods, airline crashes, and political demonstrations, and were not dedicated to reporting "news" in any sense approaching the Western one, but those versed in the small signals of policy and power changes could find far more information in them than it first appeared to a Western reader. Furthermore, comparatively more-objective reports about the outside world in newspapers and in television broadcasts, as well as fact-based rumors, foreign radio broadcasts, foreign films, publications of restricted circulation, and an unprecedented number of specialized magazines, all served to mitigate the lack of "news." The presence of increased numbers of foreigners in China, as well as a limited increase in the number of telephones, also helped to spread information.

In the early 1980s, China had three basic types of newspapers: party committee newspapers on the central, provincial, district, and city levels; professional and specialized papers published by party committee offices of certain work units and political organizations; and several types of "reference news," newspapers and magazines containing domestic reports and translations of articles written by foreigners, for restricted circulation only. In 1981 there were 42 papers on the central level, 200 on regional levels, and 164 other specialized and professional papers.[1]

The *People's Daily* (circulation 5.3 million), the only central-level party paper, was controlled directly by the Ministry of Propaganda. It usually had eight pages, more than other newspapers. It had five basic functions:

1) To announce the party's "spirit" to the people. The *People's Daily* was a vehicle for high party leaders to communicate policies rapidly, and was far more commonly employed than radio, which generally repeated newspaper articles, or television, which was not widespread enough to be effective. *People's Daily* articles were sometimes signed "Special Commentator," which people recognized to mean the author was either one of the very highest Central Committee leaders or a high-ranking party theorist. Sometimes articles reported on a meeting in general terms without publicizing the actual texts of speeches and documents, as when Deng Liqun and Peng Zhen conveyed the spirit of the 12th Party Committee as a way of launching the campaign against spiritual pollution.

2) To announce plans for a specific campaign. Selections of party documents were printed in full, so they could be studied and their principles mastered in political study meetings.

3) To filter foreign news. Each day there was a page of international news; other newspapers (with the exception of the "reference" publications) were restricted to reprinting international items from the *People's Daily*. This centralized system was an extremely effective way of controlling most people's access to information about the rest of the world.

4) To reduce conflict between the people and the party bureaucrats. As previously discussed, one form of appeal available to the Chinese was to write letters to newspapers. Newspapers also sent journalistic investigating teams to trouble spots, as in the Hunan University case.

5) To serve as a site for party struggle. Control of newspapers could pass from the hands of one faction to another. Depending on who held the chief editorships, articles expressed the views of one faction or another. In late 1983 and early 1984, for example, many front-page *People's Daily* ar-

ticles appeared in support of the reform group's party rectification, providing models for imitation or showing negative examples to prove the necessity of the purge. In the February 8, 1984, issue the exposé writer Liu Binyan published a piece on how Heilongjiang Province cadres were trying to avoid and oppose the rectification.

Each provincial party committee had a provincial newspaper under its direct control. Examples included the *Hunan Daily*, the *Southern Daily* (*Nanfang Ribao*) from Guangzhou, Hubei Province's *Yangtse Daily* (*Changjiang Ribao*), and the papers from the three province-level cities, Shanghai, Beijing, and Tianjin, such as Shanghai's *Wenhuibao* and *Liberation Daily* (*Jiefang Ribao*) and Beijing's *Beijing Evening News* (*Beijing Wanbao*). The provincial party committees' propaganda department heads or vice-heads were often the chief editors of such papers, and the power to determine editorials lay not with the paper's editorial board but with the provincial propaganda departments, which were usually located in the party committees in different parts of the city. The first and international pages of such newspapers varied little from those of the *People's Daily*. Other contents included more local information on provincial political, economic, cultural, and educational work, on the lives of local intellectuals, and on important local meetings. Such papers had the ability to transmit the policies and spirit of the provincial party committees, such as a drive to plant trees province-wide, and in this sense were relatively independent of the top level. The letters columns were also comparatively independent, and could often be more interesting than those in the *People's Daily*. For example, letters complaining of the female infanticide that followed stricter enforcement of the one-child policies were more likely to appear in provincial newspapers. Thus criticisms could be expressed on this level, although the power of such papers to resolve problems was more limited than that of top-level papers.

District- and city-level papers, such as the *Guangzhou Evening News* or the *Hengyang Daily*, were controlled by district- and city-level propaganda bureaus, and contained even more local stories. However, their principal functions were still to propagate the party's spirit and policies and educate people in proper thought. Their critical articles were apt to use the central line to criticize local practices inconsistent with current policies as a means of pressuring recalcitrant officials.

In the larger cities, some professional units such as science organizations, agricultural groups, or family planning offices had newspapers published by their resident party committees. These were not necessarily daily papers. Their articles demonstrated how to apply party policies to the lives and work of the people of that work unit. As the economic reformers progressed, they contained a greater percentage of practical information. Political organizations, such as the Communist Youth League, which ran *China Youth Daily*, and some military commands, such as that of the Guangzhou Military District, which ran *Soldier Newspaper* (*Zhanshi Bao*), also represented the voice of the party in regional and specific terms.

There were three kinds of "reference" publications, the word "reference" implying, in Professor Andrew J. Nathan's well-chosen words, "raw facts not subjected to ideological processing and not necessarily expressing the correct political attitude."[2] The first, called *Reference News* (*Cankao Xiaoxi*) and nicknamed "small reference," had in the early 1980s a circulation of 8.5 million, far greater than that of the *People's Daily*. Run by the New China News Agency and the Ministry of Foreign Affairs, both under the leadership of the State Council, it was the most trusted of China's papers.

Anyone could subscribe, although before the Cultural Revolution it had been restricted to officials of rank thirteen and above. Foreigners, however, in a loosely enforced regulation, were not allowed to see it, perhaps because the Chinese had not signed the International Copyright Convention, or perhaps because Chinese authorities preferred that foreigners not see the heavy editing of their articles. In his research, Professor Nathan discovered that *Reference News* was studied most closely of all publications by nearly half the Chinese he interviewed, and that "even people who were not deeply interested in foreign affairs enjoyed reading articles free of obvious bias." Some believed they could detect trends in Chinese policy by examining which kinds of articles were selected for reprinting.[3]

The far more restricted *Reference Materials* (*Cankao Ziliao*), or "big reference," was published twice a day in magazinelike format, with large characters because the high-ranking cadres who were permitted to see it tended to be old men with failing eyesight. Only officials of the rank of bureau chief and above, and members of their staffs, were permitted access, and the articles were less selectively reprinted, containing domestic as well as foreign news. News about political defections overseas or democratic activities within China were likely to appear in *Reference Materials* but not in *Reference News*.

A third, top-secret type of reference material, *Internal Reference* (*Nei Can*), or "red reference" (after its red headlines), was available to the highest leaders of the party only. It was usually issued in a four-to-eight page format as information became available, and was intended to inform the Central Committee and the handful of people in each province ranked high enough to read it. It was written by party members or by highly trusted non–party members (in either the New China News Agency or the various regional papers) and contained information on such sensitive matters as child-selling, major droughts and floods, and other subjects considered detrimental to the nation's socialist spirit.

Newspaper editors usually got their news by waiting for documents and articles to be transmitted to them for publication; local news was gathered by their own reporters. Each party newspaper had a New China News Agency branch, which was a local arm of the Central Committee; its journalists shared the offices of the provincial propaganda departments (not usually located in the provincial newspaper offices) or stationed in their own independent buildings. In each district, county, and province there was a communications station (*tongxun zhan*), where news would be gathered and passed upward to the newspapers. Furthermore, in each unit and commune there were propaganda groups that had special correspondents who wrote reports for higher propaganda organizations or for newspapers, and these groups were available as contact points for newspaper and New China News Agency reporters. If a reporter wished to investigate any local news story, he generally went first to the local propaganda official, who became in effect his local guide and informant. Articles were often written jointly by reporters from higher levels and by local reporters or propaganda cadres. In this fashion, the party had a way to get information about every corner of the country.

Magazines were generally a far better source of information than the newspapers. In the early 1980s, they flourished in unprecedented numbers, as almost every artists' association, research institution, publishing house, and university had its own publication. Magazines were as specialized as *Hairstyle* (*Faxing*) or *New Sports* (*Xin Tiyu*). Such publications as *World Knowledge* (*Shijie Zhishi*) and *Geography* (*Dili*) focused on faraway places and extended readers' knowledge of them. Although in name all of these magazines were published by the party, their contents were closely connected with their titles and were full of concrete information.

The famous journal *Red Flag*, which provided the theory behind various party policies, expressed the direct voice of the Central Committee. In 1983 it was controlled by fairly orthodox leaders. Each provincial party committee also had its theoretical publication, which sometimes reprinted articles from *Red Flag*. The provincial theory journals explained how the central level's "spirit" applied, in ideological terms, to local conditions. Only the most astute "decoders" (to use Professor Nathan's term) took any interest in them, for they were exceedingly dull.

The early part of 1983 was a time of reform in newspaper publishing as in other fields. *People's Daily* director Hu Jiwei's late 1982 speech on reforms was approved by his paper's editorial board and was called "Decision on Opinions on Improving Newspaper Propaganda in 1983."[4] Although most of his six-point plan was predictable enough (the *People's Daily*, as the authoritative representative of the Chinese Communist party, should quickly report on the new socialist man, be a friend to cadres in their work and study, improve page one, and so on), his sixth point, that the newspaper should publish more opinions and criticisms from the masses, led to greater publicity about the plight of intellectuals during the first months of the year, and probably had something to do with Hu Jiwei's sudden "retirement" during the campaign against spiritual pollution. In fact, Hu had pursued his policy of exposing corruption, abuses of privilege by officials, waste, nepotism, and resistance to change much earlier: in 1980, under his leadership, the *People's Daily* had exposed the fraudulent figure-fixing of the model agricultural brigade Dazhai; the cover-up of the sinking of Bohai No. 2, an offshore oil rig (the article led to the resignation of an oil minister); and the minister of commerce's habit of treating himself to lavish banquets on public money (there was another resignation).[5] Hu had continued to defend his policy of criticism/self-criticism until Document No. 7 was transmitted in early 1981. The document, "Decision on the Present Propaganda Policy for Magazines, Newspapers, and Broadcasting," called for less exposé reporting, and for criticisms to be directed at general tendencies rather than at individuals.[6] Even so, the beginning of 1983 saw a renewed aggressiveness on the part of the *People's Daily* in uncovering foot-dragging in the application of policies favorable to intellectuals. Such criticisms were directed not at the very highest leaders, but at recalcitrant middle- and lower-level cadres seen as obstructing the reformers' modernization drive.

The desire for reform was expressed by many other leaders as well. On March 5, *News Front* (*Xinwen Zhanxian*) invited representatives from newspapers in six provinces to discuss the question.[7] One complained that leftist influence was still strong; there were many limits on what could be reported, and the papers were narrow and dull. Less propaganda and more real news, including criticism, entertainment, and social articles would be better. Another leader said reporters were too passive, waiting for news to come to them rather than going out to investigate the lives of the people. An editor from Heilongjiang Province in the North said there was too great a distance between party leaders and the masses. He pointed out that professional, specialized newspapers were more popular than central party papers; *Market Newspaper* (*Shichang Bao*), on current products and prices, was extremely well liked. Many provincial papers had circulations of only 1 percent of the population, and subscribers were primarily the party committee offices of work units. His own provincial paper had a circulation of 3,100,000 copies, but fewer than 11 percent went to individual subscribers. One wealthy peasant subscribed to eight newspapers, but none of them was a party paper. Although the New China News Agency provided 30,000 words of news to the provinces per day, many papers preferred not to use those articles: in the Heilongjianq editor's paper, for example, only 30 percent of the news came from the central level.

Another problem that confronted the newspaper world was a lack of trained personnel. According to a talk by Propaganda Chief Deng Liqun on May 31, 1983,[8] only 5,000 new news workers had been trained since 1949. In the entire country, only sixteen places existed for educating journalists, and there were a total of only 364 journalism teachers. In 1983 there were 1,182 students waiting to graduate, 103 graduate students, and 220 students undergoing retraining.

In the first half of 1983, then, one of the ways newspapers carried out Hu Jiwei's reforms was through numerous features on intellectuals. According to an August summary published in *News Front*,[9] from January to June the first pages and science and education pages of the *People's Daily* published more than three hundred articles about intellectuals, 80 percent in praise of their achievements and the rest criticizing those who still persecuted them. Four main cases were taken on, the first being the Hunan University affair. One of the others dealt with the persecution to death of a Beijing No. 7 Chemical Industry Factory assistant head, another with the Hengyang Gasoline Factory in Hunan, where an engineer named Jiang Yongxu complained that because of his foreign relatives, his knowledge and skills had been persistently underused. The fourth case was the discrimination against intellectuals by the leaders of the

Guangxi Art Academy. Six frightened professors had come
to the *People's Daily* offices in person, their letters of protest
hidden in their clothing. The party committee members at
the academy were all leftists who had come to power during the Cultural Revolution. They were still threatening
intellectuals with rightist labels, and after one teacher
complained when she discovered the vice–party secretary's
daughter cheating on the entrance examinations, she was so
harassed that she was driven to a nervous breakdown.[10]

The *People's Daily* was under considerable pressure to pro-
ceed more cautiously, and the letters published were few in
number. Still, the few that made it into print were an encouragement to many readers. Other developments, such as
the extensions of the responsibility system and the debates
on humanism and alienation, also contributed to the liveli-
ness of the newspapers in the early part of 1983. However,
the newspapers were also a central force behind the campaign against spiritual pollution. Indeed, part of the problem with the movement was that it was waged largely
through papers which printed reports on the "spirit" of
meetings, rather than through formal documents transmitted down the bureaucratic ranks. Had documents been
used, the phrase "spiritual pollution" could not have been
so generally and wildly interpreted. In any case, for two
months articles on the campaign appeared in the *People's
Daily* (and hence in the other party papers) nearly every
day, covering meetings, self-criticisms, and editorials and
speeches on the need to eradicate the pollution. The most
significant signs that the winds at the newspaper had shifted
were Director Hu Jiwei's retirement (he was said to be old
enough, but the November 1983 date cannot have been co-
incidental), and the transfer away of the important liberal
theorist, Wang Ruoshui, who had written many influential
columns.[11]

The leftist trend in newspaper work reached a 1983 climax as December 26, the ninetieth anniversary of the birth of Chairman Mao, approached. In Changsha, capital of Mao's home province Hunan, a "National Discussion Meeting" of more than 130 people from various news organizations emphasized the newspapers' propaganda function and their need to uphold party principles.[12] Central Propaganda Ministry News Bureau Chief Zhong Peizhang conveyed Propaganda Chief Deng Liqun's hopes for the meeting: News workers should study the book *Chairman Mao's Directives on News Work*, use Chairman Mao's news theory to carry out the party's propaganda work, eradicate spiritual pollution, report on the experiences of "advanced" people and units, and propagandize spiritual and material civilization. The meeting was a clear warning to people in news work that the weather had gotten very chilly and that a few additional layers of protective clothing were needed; still most knew from experience that the chill would probably be a temporary one.

Radio, in the early 1980s the chief source of information in most areas of the countryside, was structured much as the newspapers were, with a Central People's Radio Station, which supplied broadcasts to the entire country, and provincial and local stations, which supplemented the central news with local reports. Most work units had loudspeakers, set up during the Cultural Revolution to announce major events in the movement and provide direction for Mao-worship activities. These broadcasted news and music, including exercise music, four or five times a day in most units. They signaled wake-up time, breakfast, lunch, after-lunch nap wake-up, and dinner. In schools, universities, and some work units, there were also mid-morning exercise interludes. Units used a mixture of central and provincial broadcasting station reports, records, and special articles read by members of the work units, preferably people with standard Northern accents. If there was an unusual announcement of an important political decision, loudspeakers all over China would sound at virtually the same moment. The loudspeakers could also be used in emergency situations to alert people to flood or fire, and to mobilize them for rescue work. Although most Chinese were used to the regimentation of their lives by loudspeaker, early-morning broadcasts could be a tremendous intrusion. One professor we know used to reach out his window and cut the wire, but it was always repaired again within a few days.

Although in the early 1980s television sets were being purchased in extraordinary numbers, the channels and contents were still quite limited. Most people could get two channels on their sets, the Central People's Television Station and their provincial channel. Residents of Guangdong Province near Hong Kong set up antennae to receive Hong Kong stations, but these were periodically outlawed until the mood loosened and they could go up again (in Shenzhen on the border, a new television station was struggling to provide attractive alternative programming to Hong Kong's sex, violence, and Cantonese-language shows).[13] Chinese stations generally began their broadcasts in the late afternoon with mathematics and English-language programs, then a half hour of news (including some international news broadcast by satellite arrangement with U.S. and British networks), and then the featured program, often an evening-length film, sporting event, or performance of dance, music, opera, or a play. The broadcast day was over when the show ended, usually around 10:30 or 11:00. Some foreign films were shown, generally the same ones as those shown in movie theaters. There were also short travelogues on other countries, serials such as "The Man from Atlantis," which was a huge hit, and frequent coverage of foreign performers visiting China.

In early 1983, as a result of a March 31 to April 11 meeting held in Beijing,[14] a News Center was established to oversee the work of the three major stations, the Central People's Radio Station, the Central People's Television Station, and the China International Broadcasting Station (Radio Beijing). The purpose of the center was to ensure that the stations uphold a socialist direction and "use patriotic and Communist thought as a central content for arranging programs."

"Reform" for the broadcast industries was said to mean an emphasis on "freshness, speed, brevity, scope, and loudness." It was still considered necessary to emphasize the Four Basic Principles through "proletarian journalism"; without these principles, reform was said to be impossible.[15] Within these limits, however, even in the chillier months of 1983, programs were comparatively varied and the contents more oriented to audience tastes.

With the campaign against spiritual pollution, a "National Broadcasting and Television Propaganda Work Meeting" was organized in Beijing. Such pollution was called a major problem in broadcasting.[16] Programmers should promote the Five Stresses, Four Beauties, and Three Ardent Loves, and oppose bourgeois liberalism. The chief of the Broadcast and Television Bureau, Wu Lengxi, called on over 200,000 professionals to "study the directives earnestly." Wu described spiritual pollution in more specific terms when, on December 1, he said that some broadcasters put on "gray-colored" programs, making up stories that distorted revolutionary history.[17] Some programs, Wu said, fostered a mood of hopelessness and cynicism to satisfy the tastes of a small number of people. Programmers put on foreign shows indiscriminately, he said, including some influenced by bourgeois ideas and life styles. Stations sought to draw viewers and sell more advertisements, "looking toward money in everything"; the directors of certain series tried too hard for laughs and grossly imitated the West, allowing performers to dress up in Western clothing and behave in a casual Western manner. Female performers especially were said to take advantage of playing negative characters in order to make provocative gestures on stage.

Toward the conclusion of the movement, at a December 28 meeting of the Ministry of Culture and the Ministry of Radio and Television Broadcasting, Propaganda Chief Deng Liqun placed broadcasting outside the sphere that was said to be most seriously affected by spiritual pollution. Still, it was only natural that television writers and directors would limit themselves more narrowly, to avoid bringing trouble to themselves and their families, and that television and radio programming would become, in the short term at least, less outspoken and interesting.

In the early 1980s, the principal publishing houses in China were the People's Publishing Houses under the Ministry of Culture and the Central Propaganda Ministry. There were also a number of more specialized houses, such as the Children's Publishing House (*Shaonian Ertong Chubanshe*), China Youth Publishing House (*Zhongguo Qingnian Chubanshe*, under the Communist Youth League), China Social Sciences Publishing House (*Zhongguo Shehui Kexue Chubanshe*), China Antiquities Publishing House (*Zhongguo Guji Chubanshe*), People's Literature Publishing House (*Renmin Wenxue Chubanshe*), and so on. Some branches of writers' and artists' associations also had their own houses, such as the Flower City Publishing House (*Huacheng Chu-*

banshe) under the Guangdong Province Writers' Association, as did certain work units such as the Chinese Academy
of Social Sciences and Wuhan University. According to 1981
statistics, there were then 111 publishing houses at the central
level and 103 at various regional levels. (This number has
been rapidly increasing.)[18]

Most publishing houses were controlled through an annual meeting of houses held by the Central Propaganda
Ministry, at which they received a general guide on what
was to be published during the year, and in what proportions (more revolutionary history, for example, fewer detective novels). On January 8, 1983, a meeting called for a broad
patriotic effort to uphold the Four Basic Principles. In accordance with reforms, publishing-house workers should be
younger and more professional; techniques and management should be upgraded. However, party guidance of publishing should be strengthened.[19]

All bookstores in China were part of a single system, the
New China Bookstores. Every city, according to its size, had
at least a small store. A few bookshops specialized in foreign
languages or in ethnic minority questions (including books
about minorities and those written in minority languages).
Despite the comparatively large number of stores, however,
getting a specific book was a constant problem. Popular
books quickly sold out, distribution was exceedingly un-
even, and even a map of one's home province could be hard
to obtain.

In early 1983 a meeting was held on reform of the distribution of books.[20] Under discussion was how to change the
relationship between bookstores and publishing houses and
how to increase the number of retail outlets so as to reach
more readers. The contract system was already being carried
out experimentally in some areas. One way to increase the
branches in the single-bookstore system was to permit col-

lectively and individually run (as opposed to state-run) outlets. With the new flexibility, it was said that the number of
bookstores by 1983 had increased five times over that of 1981
(when there had been 9,366 bookstores). The new system
had also solved the problem of over 109,000 young people
"waiting for work." Furthermore, it had brought books to
the countryside: more than 60,000 "representative selling
sites" (*daixiao dian*) had appeared, making books available
together with such necessities as soap and toothpaste. In
Jilin Province's Changchun, one collectively run branch of
the New China Bookstore signed a contract, dating from
January 1983, to sell books at the railroad station. Because
the workers had an incentive, it remained open beyond the
usual eight hours. Young workers could choose to sell what
was popular, and hence could increase sales. In a single
month, even after salaries, bonuses, and expenses, the outlet
was able to turn over 1,500 yuan to the mother store.

A persistent problem in publishing and bookselling since
1949 had been the system whereby if books were not sold,
the store, not the publishing house, bore the loss. If a book
sold out, the publisher had little incentive to reprint it. Publishing had little to do with the market, and everything to
do with the state plan. With the reforms, this began to
change. Bookstores and publishing houses began to work
more closely together. A bookstore could choose whether
or not to order a book, and it could place orders all over
the country by mail, not confining its products to books
only from the center and their own local publishing houses.
Publishing houses could also open their own sales outlets,
so that if the New China Bookstores did not sell or order
their books, they could try to do so on their own.

In 1983, however, market forces were not to be permitted
to take over altogether. In July of that year Chen Hansheng,
a scholar from the Chinese Academy of Social Sciences,

wrote to Central Committee leaders to complain about distribution. The Commercial Printing House (*Shangwu Yinshua Guan*) had invited him to edit a series of books on foreign history, which had proved very popular with young people. The copies sold were very few, however, since only 10,000 of each volume had been published. According to an article in the September 16 *People's Daily*, the Central Propaganda Ministry held a meeting of publishing leaders because of Chen's letter. However, it concluded that publishers should not "look to money in everything"—it was still necessary to give the young people more political books.

This more intensely ideological wind blew stronger during the campaign against spiritual pollution, when publishing houses were criticized as having relinquished party publishing principles. They had translated too many foreign books, including science fiction and books by bourgeois writers; they had revived too many old Chinese books, including some stories of martial arts gang fights, to satisfy their readers. Paper was scarce (ever since the massive deforestations of the Great Leap Forward in 1958) and of poor quality—the party considered it a pity to waste paper on "bad" books. Publishing plans should not cater only to the desires of young people, since their "thought" and world views were unstable. Instead, publishers had a responsibility to help them change their ideas and love socialism.

During the campaign, the China Youth Publishing House was held up as a model. On November 13 the *People's Daily* published an article entitled "They Upheld the Correct Publishing Direction," emphasizing the house's contribution to educating young people in patriotic Communist thought. The house was praised for printing 28,810,000 copies of a new book, *Speech on the History of the Chinese Communist Party*. When other houses were printing detective stories, old works, and Western novels, the China Youth Publishing House was printing materials on revolutionary struggles, heroes and peasant uprisings.

On December 3, 1983, the Publishing Bureau's chief, Bian Chungang, wrote that the publishing world was an important channel for promulgating Marxism–Leninism–Mao Zedong Thought and for carrying out Communist education.[21] According to him, writers and editors had a heavy responsibility for the construction of socialist spiritual civilization. To do this, it was necessary to increase the publication of books on political thought education. He announced that sixty books on the works of Lenin were to be reprinted, and also soon to come out was a collection of letters by Chairman Mao, *Basic Readings in Chairman Mao's Works*. Other publications on Zhou Enlai, Liu Shaoqi, Chen Yun, and other revolutionary leaders were planned; so were works on and by North Korea's Kim Il Sung, Romania's Ceausescu, and Yugoslavia's Tito.

In contrast with publishing, which, despite paper restrictions and censorship, was in the early 1980s quite developed in China, public libraries were rare. According to a 1983 *People's Daily* report, in 1949 there had been only 55 libraries in the whole country. By 1981, from the county level up, there were 1,787, but one-third of all the counties had no libraries, and certain entire provinces had none. The ratio of libraries to people was 1 to 55,000.

Public libraries were generally open only to those who had letters of introduction from their work units or residence committees. After a long wait, a library card might be issued. Usually, even with the card, only some books could be borrowed. Many books did not appear on index cards, particularly if they were foreign, from Taiwan, or "internal." If, by chance, an ordinary person heard of the existence of such a book and wanted to look at it, he would probably be asked to supply proof of why he needed it (usually because of the nature of his work), then he had to go to the party leaders of the library to try to get their approval, then wait for their office to notify the borrowing office. Such complicated bureaucratic procedures were a major deterrent to anyone who hoped to read something a little out of the ordinary.

A similar system usually operated in the libraries and reading rooms of work units: there was "open" borrowing and "internal" borrowing. In some universities, "internal" books were available to teachers but not to students, with graduate students permitted to examine them on site. Many officials of rank thirteen and above (the so-called "high-ranking cadres") had special cards that entitled them to see all books. Furthermore, if a library received new "internal" books, the officials were often notified of their arrival. According to the orthodox party viewpoint, the higher a person's rank, the greater his ability to resist polluting ideas. In practice, however, clearance to look at "internal" materials was one of the many special privileges accorded to high-ranking officials. (This notion of resistance to pollution applied in film viewing as well. High cadres were often allowed to see films before ordinary people, and they often saw foreign films that were never shown in ordinary theaters. "Internal film" tickets were thus highly coveted, an excellent gift for "going through the back door.") In some cities, internal books were available in New China Bookstores. There were sometimes entire bookstores set aside for this purpose, or a separate room might be designated which ordinary people were not permitted to enter. There might also be rooms which were open to Chinese but closed to foreigners. Foreign journalists and scholars were often tantalized by the hope of seeing some of these materials, only to be disappointed when they realized that some of the most mundane materials were classified in China.

In the early 1980s, as today, policies of openness to the West but frequently tight domestic ideological controls created a contradictory, often confusing situation for Chinese people with regard to foreigners and the outside world. This conflict was reflected in their still-limited access to information about other countries and in restrictions governing contact with foreigners within China. Internally, continual fluctuations between tightness and looseness also forced Chinese to play a continuous guessing game. Sometimes, for example, foreign-Chinese contact was quite unrestricted, while at other times people who had extensive unofficial contacts with foreigners were called to account by their leaders or subjected to other pressures. The situation varied from province to province, even from unit to unit, depending on the attitudes of local party leaders. In some areas, Chinese had to ask their leaders for permission to talk with foreign teachers, students, or business people, or to invite them to their homes; when the visit was over, a report had to be made. In other places, no such measures were required, although the Chinese who extended their friendship and hospitality were aware that they were taking a risk. Contacts with journalists and diplomats were, as to be expected, monitored much more closely than those with teachers, students, and business people. Journalists and diplomats had greater difficulty traveling within China, having to apply for internal visas when they wished to leave Beijing, while other foreigners were free to visit any of over a hundred cities without special permission, including all the major ones.

With the exception of pornography, foreign-language books could be carried or shipped in from abroad with relatively little censorship (if something was confiscated, intended either for a Chinese or a foreigner, a notice was sent to the addressee to that effect). That such books entered so freely was sometimes because few customs officers had foreign-language skills. Chinese materials were generally more closely checked. In fact, when people went through customs in Guangzhou there were separate procedures for foreign nationals, Hong Kong and Macao Chinese, and Chinese citizens. Hong Kong and Macao Chinese were often treated rudely and subjected to thorough searches, while foreigners were usually treated with courtesy and a minimum of fuss.

In the early 1980s, resident foreign teachers and students were often quite unrestricted. With some exceptions, foreign teachers had great freedom in their choice of teaching materials. For example, one of us, Judith Shapiro, taught selections from *Catch-22, Waiting for Godot,* and a *Time* magazine article on party corruption in the Soviet Union (which applied closely to China as well). On only one occasion did department party leaders ask to review the lecture notes, when a lecture was planned on Hong Kong. The lack of surveillance may have had much to do with the fact that of the department's seven party leaders, only one knew a foreign language, and that was Russian. (In 1985, more qualified leaders were promoted.)

Chinese privileged to study or teach in university foreign-language departments where there were foreign teachers thus had an opportunity to learn directly about the outside world, and many visiting teachers built up libraries which operated on far more "open" borrowing systems than the Chinese ones did. Other Chinese had opportunities to become friendly with foreigners through their work in foreign trade, the China International Travel Service, and related occupations. For the vast majority of Chinese, however, in the early 1980s as today, foreigners remained akin to strange animals, and many, especially in the countryside, had never laid eyes on a real live one, much less spoken to one. For these people, information about the outside world came primarily through the Voice of America's Chinese- and English-language broadcasts, through international television news, *Reference News*, and foreign films. Television coverage of visiting foreign performers and sports teams was another way for Chinese to see foreigners, while Chinese performances of Western dramas, translations of numerous volumes of Western literature, and some Western dance offered further exposure to Western ideas and aesthetics. Letters to and from the outside world, once sufficient cause for long imprisonment or even execution, were able to pass freely. Many people who had relatives in Taiwan began to communicate again after a break of more than thirty years, using intermediaries in Hong Kong and other countries, and some Taiwan Chinese began to visit the mainland. A person who had relatives abroad became a most desirable match or friend, since that person might have access to hard-to-buy goods and foreign currency. Letters from tourists met on the street were still, however, sometimes considered a sign of "bad thought."

As it is today, the importance of the Voice of America (and, to a lesser extent, the BBC) was inestimable. Listening was permitted, even encouraged as a way to learn English, and the VOA reached millions. (Listening to Taiwan and Soviet broadcasts was, however, illegal.) The VOA was the single most important source of information about the outside world, as well as a highly trusted source of information about what was going on within China. Many Chinese first learned of major events occurring within their own country by listening to the VOA.

Foreign films have often been selected to confirm the

worst about life abroad, although the situation is improving. One "B" film widely shown in 1980, called *Nightmare* (*Nightmare in Badham County* in the U.S.), describes the rape of a black girl by a redneck policeman, his incarceration of her and her white girlfriend in a prison camp (the judge is his relative), and the murder of one of the girls as they try to escape. Many Chinese people understood the film to be a courageous exposé of capitalist society by a filmmaker who had probably been imprisoned for speaking out. Thousands of essays were written for political study classes applauding the film and drawing the conclusion that socialism was superior to capitalism. Other films were better—Chaplin's films on the plight of the worker were perennial favorites, and *Death on the Nile* and *The Sound of Music* were extremely popular. (*Kramer vs. Kramer* and *On Golden Pond* were among more recent less political offerings.)

Many magazines and book publishers specialized in translations. The Dramatists' Association's *Foreign Drama* (*Waiguo Xiju*) published plays by Brecht, Mérimée, and O'Casey. *World Literature* (*Shijie Wenxue*), *Foreign Literature and Art* (*Waiguo Wenyi*), and Jiangsu Province's *Yilin* were also important sources for foreign works. The Foreign Language Publishing House (*Waiwen Chubanshe*), New World Publishing House (*Xin Shijie Chubanshe*), and World Languages Publishing House (*Shijieyu Chubanshe*) all put foreign literature into Chinese, while another group of publications was devoted to putting Chinese into English for foreign consumption. Among them was the China Literary Magazine Publishing House's (*Zhongguo Wenxue Zazhishe*) excellent line of Panda Books, which included translations of novels by the maligned Shen Congwen, whose writing was not easily available in Chinese editions within China. The new English-language newspaper, *The China Daily*, made impressive strides and became one of the more interesting publications about China in any language.

Until the recent multiplication of regional publications made such surveillance impossible, translations of foreign works were planned annually, with a careful balance among various countries and a consideration of the "healthiness" of the materials. It was often difficult to judge whether or not a work would be considered acceptable. Most translators, in taking on projects, tried to choose works that had a good chance of being published, and thus tended toward works critical of capitalist countries or at least neutral toward them. One student, for example, decided to translate *To Kill a Mockingbird* over the other books we recommended to him because he felt it would be the most politically acceptable. Even with this built-in slant, however, Western works could not help but give Chinese readers some sense of life on the outside.

As far as foreign contact was concerned, the tightening in the latter part of 1983 was at least partially offset by the improvement in U.S.-China relations with Caspar Weinberger's September visit, by the preparations for Premier Zhao Ziyang's visit to the U.S. in early 1984, and by the knowledge that President Reagan planned to visit China in the spring of 1985. Although members of some units were still feeling the chilly effects of the U.S. having granted political asylum to tennis player Hu Na in March, contact with foreigners seemed comparatively relaxed and untroubled when one of us, Judith Shapiro, traveled in China in September–November 1983. In general, much depended on the foreigner's understanding of the risks and responsibilities involved. If a foreigner can learn Chinese ways to the extent that he knows how and when to be discreet, friendship and frank conversation have been possible in post-Mao China even in the tightest of times.

The End of the Campaign Against Spiritual Pollution

The campaign against spiritual pollution did not last. This was not because reformers disagreed with conservatives that there was a need for tight ideological controls, but rather because overeager leftists expanded the scope of the movement beyond theoretical and literary and art circles, threatening social and economic stability. Peasants' confidence in the economic reforms was being shaken, creating potential for chaos among 80 percent of the population. Some businesses were afraid to sign contracts with foreign companies and governments lest they too be accused of spiritual pollution. Intellectuals' fears that another Cultural Revolution might be beginning created a psychological climate adverse to modernization, while artists and writers secretly sympathized with such major targets as Zhou Yang. Party leaders themselves recognized that they had never come to a consensus on the goals of the movement; it had gotten out of hand before the announced meeting to clarify policies about the ideological front had ever been held.[1]

Toward mid-November 1983 the Secretariat of the party issued an internal "Report on the Expansion of the Movement to Eliminate Spiritual Pollution," including many examples of excesses and misinterpretations.[2] In some areas of the countryside, the decollectivized family economy had come to a halt; contracts to farm government land had been torn up by zealous officials, and peasants who sold their wares in free markets had been detained by Public Security Bureau personnel. In some rural banks, the large savings deposits of peasants had been frozen, and some peasants committed suicide in the belief that their new wealth would make them targets of unbearable criticism. In urban areas, some unit leaders claimed that permanent waves were examples of spiritual pollution: hair should not be permitted to grow past the shoulders, pants legs should not be too narrow (an interdiction of blue jeans), and makeup and jewelry were forbidden. Some youths in Sichuan Province and the Northeast had donned red armbands and invaded people's homes to chop off long hair and break off the high heels of people's shoes in a manner all too reminiscent of Red Guard "search raids" during the Cultural Revolution. In the military, overenthusiastic application of the campaign was threatening unity and troop morale. Some officers had forced their men to turn in for examination all books they owned except the *Works* of Deng Xiaoping. Photographs of fiancées had been confiscated as polluting influences, and soldiers from the countryside had been forbidden to find wives in the cities, a common way for soldiers from peasant stock to upgrade their own standards of living.

After this report was received, the Politics Bureau held a meeting and issued internal documents, including talks by Hu Yaobang and Zhao Ziyang, setting limits on the campaign against spiritual pollution. Only incorrect thought in theory, literature, and art circles was to be the target. The campaign should not affect the lives of ordinary people. Nor was it to be used, as some leftists were doing, to attack the party's line and to blame existing social problems on the party under the leadership of Deng Xiaoping (a reference to the economic reforms). Open policies to the West were reaffirmed. The principal tasks now were said to be economic construction and the rectification of the party.

Following this meeting, the atmosphere began to change. An article in the November 17 *China Youth Daily*, "Pollution

Should Be Eliminated, [But] Life Should Be Beautified," deplored notions that curling hair, dancing, and wearing fashionable clothing constituted spiritual pollution. The Secretariat ordered the Ministry of Propaganda to ensure that all the newspapers in China reprinted this article. Then on November 19 Deng Liqun, author of the campaign, was quoted self-critically in an article in the *People's Daily*:

To efficiently realize the Four Modernizations, we have carried out the policy of enlivening the economy. We should not say that the unsuccessful things that have arisen in practicing the reforms of the economic system are spiritual pollution. We should not call the works which have deficiencies and faults but basically follow the right direction spiritually polluting. We should not, because of eliminating spiritual pollution, make the lives of the people dull.

This moderating note, sounded by one of China's leading conservatives, signaled a victory for the reformers, and by the beginning of December 1983 the movement was waning. At the December 8 meeting of the Standing Committee of the 6th National People's Congress (whose head was the conservative Peng Zhen), it was conceded that the question of spiritual pollution was exceedingly complex, and there should be no overly hasty decision about what to do about it.[3] On December 9 Deng Liqun said that the party had made it clear that the spiritual pollution campaign should not be waged in the countryside.[4] On December 16 it was reported that Robert Runcie, the visiting Archbishop of Canterbury, had been promised that the campaign would not affect religion.[5] On December 18 came the State Council's announcement that the campaign should leave science and technology alone.[6] Another cautionary article appeared in the December 21 *People's Daily*:

What is worth paying attention to now is that some have expanded the elimination of spiritual pollution into daily life, have

said that wearing high heels, curling hair, wearing new-style clothing, growing flowers, and so on—all things beautifying life—are
also spiritual pollution. This is wrong. People should not mix up
spiritual pollution with changes in material and cultural life, and
even more, they should not interfere excessively with different
customs of life. . . . Some comrades have also said that some theoretical questions raised in the process of our explorations of economic reform are spiritual pollution. If they bring these notions
into the countryside, it will create very serious consequences. So
the Secretariat of the Chinese Communist party is paying attention to these questions and has contacted the organizations concerned [probably the Ministry of Propaganda and the Ministry of
Culture] and told them that they must correctly and realistically
carry out propaganda. This is why there have been a series of
articles published by the *People's Daily* to explain the policies and
the limitations, and why the *China Youth Daily* editorial, "Spiritual Pollution Must Be Eliminated, [But] Life Must Be Beautified," was published. As soon as people see this, they will understand that eliminating spiritual pollution and the Cultural
Revolution are different. It is not a question of sweeping everything away, but a question of eliminating what must be eliminated, retaining what must be retained, and developing what
must be developed.

Although Western newspapers and magazines began to
report that the campaign against spiritual pollution was
over, a more careful reading of certain speeches published
toward the end of December was less reassuring. On December 18, for example, Hu Yaobang told the American
overseas-Chinese scholar Yang Liyu that the movement
would continue in critical theory and in literary and art
circles. Spiritual pollution could not be eliminated quickly,
he said. It was a slow job, to be done through education
and propaganda. It should, however, be limited to areas
delineated by the Central Committee.[7] The article in the
December 21 *People's Daily* echoed this: "The work of eliminating spiritual pollution has just begun. In the theory and

art and literature worlds, some people have not yet been gotten through to, some are still resisting."[8] On December 24 the *People's Daily* reported a November 30 speech by Politics Department Director Yu Qiuli:

To oppose spiritual pollution is a long term duty. To do this, we should have sufficient understanding and full preparation of thought. . . . Those who are involved with theory, literature and art, education, news, publishing, radio and television, the masses' culture work and the masses' political thought work, absolutely cannot be infected with spiritual pollution. This is the main point of eliminating spiritual pollution.

As the campaign against spiritual pollution disappeared from the newspapers and radio broadcasts, the party thus reserved a few crucial areas for continued monitoring and restriction. Writers and artists had been reminded once again that their main task was the inculcation of socialist values and enthusiasm for the socialist cause. Those who hoped to investigate the roots of society's ills, or who wished to express their own inner worlds, or who sought to espouse humanistic concerns for others, had received a clear warning.

III
The
1985 Spring
Wind

Continued Improvement in the Status of Intellectuals

It is often a rule of thumb in China that the better the economic situation, the warmer the climate for intellectual freedom. When the populace's material needs are satisfied, the party seems to have less fear of unrest and dissidence, and seems able to risk easing the reins on expression. This was the case during our extended visit in early 1985. However, the reforms we observed were more than a simple "loosening," more than a warming of the winds. Many of the reforms were restructuring basic relationships between rulers and ruled, as well as expanding freedom of thought and expression. Most people even tended to dismiss the campaign against spiritual pollution as an amusing memory, a temporary aberration in a trend toward increasing relaxation of personal and ideological constraints.

Under Mao, the slogan "The more educated the person, the more reactionary" summarized the anti-elitist attitudes that led to grave persecution of intellectuals. However, since his return to power in 1977 Deng Xiaoping, who was himself paraded in a dunce cap during the fanatical decade, has fought an uphill battle to stop such persecution. He began the process with the restoration of university entrance examinations in 1977. Another pressing task was the "overturning" of the criminal sentences and political "labels" of victims of repression, in many cases posthumously.

But the restoration of political honor to the victims of political campaigns has proven simpler than provision for their daily needs. In early 1985, many intellectuals still endured miserable living conditions or had not yet gained positions in which their talents could be used fully. The corruption and incompetence of local leaders was an ongoing problem, in this as in many other areas. A directive might be issued, for example, that intellectuals of a certain rank should be given gas cooking stoves; the stoves ended up in the homes of party leaders who suddenly defined themselves as intellectuals.

Such problems were gradually being rectified, however, and educated people had gained increasing control of enterprises and institutions. No longer was it necessary that all leaders be party members, and many old party leaders had been forced into retirement or into advisory positions through campaigns to rejuvenate the leadership and to "separate party and enterprise." In the interest of China's modernization drive, the party, which once caused havoc and inefficiency in its role as leader of the Chinese economy and the system of education, was being replaced in enterprises by engineers, skilled managers, and other educated people.

In arts troupes, in universities, in writers' and artists' associations, literary magazines, publishing houses, and television and radio stations, the policy of promoting skilled people to leadership positions meant that for the first time since before the Cultural Revolution, most of those making decisions about the day-to-day operations of a work unit had relevant expertise. Those under their control were less subject to demands for inane revisions and time-consuming political meetings; managers were free to emphasize production over indoctrination, although the new leaders, like the leaders of the past, were still responsible for the political "correctness" of their unit's work.

Now that enterprises had to demonstrate economic self-sufficiency there was intense interest in Western managerial techniques. Because some unprofitable factories and shops were being closed and jobs lost, China's reformers also felt an urgent need to learn about social security and welfare systems for the unemployed. Access to information about the West had become, in the view of some reformers, the most essential element in the success of China's modernization program. The greater the intellectual exchange with the outside world, the more alternatives China would have to the limited experience it had known to date, and the better equipped it would be to find solutions to its problems.

We found similar interest in Western legal experience, particularly in contract and international law; from peasants to import-export corporations, the Chinese were learning that they had to protect themselves to function effectively in the modern world. There was also great desire to know how private universities were run, and to understand a system of employment based on recommendations, personal interviews, and job performance. Even private foundations were considered worth learning about, for China's most affluent peasants had already begun to donate funds for the public good.

Freedom to Choose Occupation and Residence; Freedom to Travel

Waste of talent was once one of the more obvious consequences of the system of forcible assignment of jobs by the party. Many people worked in occupations which they neither did well nor were happy in. In Deng's China, the emphasis on the contribution of intellectuals has led to the gradual recognition that the problem of underuse of talent may be resolved by increasing the freedoms of skilled personnel to negotiate their own jobs.

As of 1985 such liberties were extended in particular to technicians, engineers, and managers, but other less skilled people, too, had gained in freedom. To cure the crippling problem of overstaffing—in many work units, as many as half the people on the payroll were superfluous—excess workers were encouraged to find their own jobs, or they were simply dismissed. Unfortunately, good workers who preferred to be elsewhere did not yet have such mobility: over and over again one heard the complaint, "My unit will not release me."

The residence card system remained a constraint on increased professional mobility. Residence cards were still necessary to procure annual ration coupons that permitted people to buy necessities such as grain. Because of the tremendous overcrowding in the large cities, the Public Security Bureau only rarely approved someone's transfer from a small town "up" to a larger one. In a common situation, an individual had an attractive job offer, the old unit had consented to a "release," but the new unit was unable to persuade Public Security to transfer the residence card. Transfers to Beijing and Shanghai, with their high living standards, were particularly difficult to arrange. Without a "back door," or a personal connection greased with gifts and favors, such moves were all but impossible.

But even the constricting force of the residence card had eased. With many free markets, plenty of goods, and readily available black-market ration coupons, the residence card no longer necessarily determined residence. Large numbers of housekeepers from the countryside, for the most part young peasant girls drawn by city life, were taken in and supported entirely by the now wealthier urban families. The government permitted this, even encouraged it, by providing centers for introduction, with no questions about residence cards asked. Peasants were permitted to relocate to the very largest cities for only a short time, but occupational and residential mobility was probably greater than it had been at any time since the Revolution. In a strategy that was one of the building blocks of the economic reforms, those who showed special entrepreneurial talent were encouraged to move permanently to the small county seats and towns to build factories, hotels, and restaurants; to trade in goods from other provinces; and to expand the service industry that remained one of the Chinese economy's weakest sectors.

Economic reforms had also led to much greater freedom to travel, and a greater incentive to do so. With the expansion of the private-sector economy, individual entrepreneurs could go to other cities to purchase goods for resale, activities previously often called "smuggling." Where once a letter of introduction from a work unit had been necessary to stay overnight in a hotel, now the showing of a work I.D. was usually sufficient. In some small hotels run by individuals (frequently just extra space in a family room) even an

I.D. was often unnecessary. So many people were on the road that the passenger and transport systems were over-strained to the point of crisis: a new black market in train tickets was flourishing, and long-distance buses packed people in like sacks of flour.

The issuance of passports for travel abroad, too, had "loosened" to the extent that U.S. consular officials told us that they felt that the Chinese now seemed to be leaving most of the decisions to them. American visas were ex-tremely hard to come by: a Chinese had to "prove" to the officer's satisfaction that he or she would return, and many married just before they applied so that the Americans would be satisfied that there were hostages binding them to China. Those returning from abroad were warmly wel-comed, and seemed better utilized than they had been some years ago, when uneducated party leaders often treated the first returnees with suspicion and made it difficult for them to apply what they had learned. Indeed, Chinese could get free plane tickets home if they needed them, and those re-turning often received plum jobs in major cities like Beijing.

New Freedoms for Workers and Peasants

In most areas of the countryside, personal freedoms had expanded to include: freedom from abuse by local of-ficials and freedom to complain about them; freedom to determine how time is to be spent; freedom to engage in a wide range of economic activities; freedom (in some cases) to choose local representatives; freedom from hunger and the fear of it; and freedom to travel and to move to small towns. All were, in some measure, a consequence of the economic reforms.

Under the tremendously successful "responsibility system," land previously farmed collectively by "production teams" had been divided among the peasant families according to the number of family members and their labor power. This return of collectivized land to family control is one of the most radical reforms ever to have taken place in a Communist society. Families could plant how and when they wished: local officials had lost the despotic power to control the number of "work points" (and hence the amount of grain) a peasant earned for a day's work. No longer did peasants have to produce a banquet if an official showed up at their home; no longer did they fear beatings and starvation if they incurred the leaders' displeasure. The old production teams had been disbanded, leaving only "villagers' groups," the heads of which were, in some areas, elected democratically by the peasants themselves.

With the unleashing of individual incentives, crop yields in most areas were enormous. Government warehouses were filled to overflowing and there was food enough to cover years of natural disasters. Indeed, there was so much food that the government eliminated the quotas of grain each family had to produce, purchasing it, at a low price, only if peasants could not find more lucrative private markets. Peasants were exhorted to turn to other money-making occupations. "Specialized households" engaged in a single activity such as pig-raising or growing medicinal plants were generally more prosperous than traditional grain farmers. The slogan "Leave the earth but not the land" conveyed the reformers' vision of a rural population no longer made up of peasants.

In 1985, only the one-child policy could be said to have reduced some freedoms, and this constraint was felt to be a far greater hardship in the countryside than it was in the cities. While urban wives, too, had to contend with husbands' and relatives' preference for boys, for rural families the production of male children was seen as an economic necessity. There was a clear correlation between labor power and wealth in the countryside; the more working males in a family, the more land it would be assigned under the "responsibility system." And, with the elimination of some of the collective social guarantees, couples with only female children, who almost always married away, often faced great poverty and loneliness in their old age. Thus the economic reforms conflicted directly with the official policy of limiting births, and with the imperative need for population control in China. But in other areas, personal freedom in the countryside had vastly expanded. Furthermore, since peasants were free to earn money they were beginning to appreciate the value of skills and information, and, in some instances, were finding ways to train themselves in agronomy and business. In this way, the economic reforms were creating a new breed of better-educated peasant who might, with time, develop demands for greater political participation and for even greater personal freedom.

In the cities and towns, the new system as applied to economic enterprises was designed to allow qualified people to make decisions on how production was to be organized, on what was to be manufactured after the primary contract with the government was fulfilled, and, to some degree, on what salaries were to be paid to employees. The overall effect was to raise workers' morale. In many units, managers were now elected by the workers themselves. They held office for a set term. In principle at least, if they performed poorly they would not be reelected. Workers generally voted in their workshops or their political study meetings to choose representatives to a committee, which in turn selected the manager; in one factory, we were told, the campaign was "as exciting as your elections for president." The elected manager had authority to appoint vice-managers and workshop leaders; he gave them contracts for a specific term of years. The new system in the cities as in the countryside thus marked a fundamental change in the working relationship between ruler and ruled. Workers had the power to change their leaders. Complaints, even open disagreement with managers, had become common.

There were, nevertheless, still many imperfections in the new system. Some of the new leaders were said to be little better than the old. With only a limited time to arrange better housing for themselves, to find good jobs for their relatives, and to enjoy the privileges of rank, they now hastened to pay attention to matters that were of less urgent concern to their tenured predecessors. Furthermore, some managers protected the interests of the workers who had elected them over the interests of the state. Tax evasion grew widespread, and the lavish bonuses issued at the end of 1984 often did not reflect the true financial worth of many enterprises. Some policy makers who were intrigued by Western practices mentioned to us the need for a system of "checks and balances" among managers, union, and advisory board (a group usually made up of retired leaders).

The new system was, of course, still experimental: the reform of the cities began officially only in October 1984, and in early 1985 was proceeding unevenly. Most workers already, however, appeared far more interested in quality and productivity than they had been during the Cultural Revolution. It had become common for stocks and corporation shares to be sold to workers, giving them a stake in the results of their work. Some enterprises in Guangdong Province and in Shanghai had even raised capital by selling shares to the public.

Belief, Expression, and Political Participation

By the mid-1980s, much of the cynicism that character-ized young people immediately following the Cultural Rev-olution, particularly among the ex–Red Guard generation that grew up with such high expectations of socialism, had at last abated. The atmosphere was more optimistic now that living standards were rising and personal freedom had expanded. There was more freedom of expression in ordi-nary conversation; much of the nervousness about "small reports" to superiors was gone, and open dispute with lead-ers was not uncommon. We witnessed one noisy argument between some dancers and a troupe leader who was trying to force the dancers to take a class with a less popular in-structor. It is unlikely that such a vocal dispute could have occurred even two years earlier.

A greater degree of political dissent was also tolerated. The old non-Communist parties, such as the Democratic party, and other groups made up of intellectuals, groups of returned overseas Chinese, and ex–Guomindang (KMT) members, which had become useless during the Cultural Revolution, once again had substantive roles to play as gatherers and transmitters of opinion, thereby influencing national policy. Membership in these non-Communist par-ties had increased, and they were trying to enroll young people.

The April 1985 meetings of the People's Political Consul-tative Conference, which had had little or no impact on real affairs, were far livelier than similar meetings held in previous years. Dissent was openly expressed over such basic party principles as Marx's judgment that religion is an opiate of the people. Policy makers in general were taking the suggestions of intellectuals seriously, in accordance with the official policy of emphasizing the contribution of intellectuals to the modernization program. Many intellectuals had been enrolled in the policy-making apparatus itself; they did research connected with the recent reforms and they helped prepare documents concerned with important policies. Activists who had taken part in the autumn 1980 democratic election movement in the universities were often, in punishment, given demeaning job assignments on graduation, but many of them had now managed to find their way back into positions that were productive and even powerful. For example, one free-thinking friend of ours had been appointed to the municipal party committee of one of Hunan's largest cities.

Expansion of political participation had occurred to some degree within the Communist party itself. Local party branch leaders were now elected directly by party members within the work units, although the most important leaders, including members of provincial, municipal, district, and county party committees, were still appointed by the party from top to bottom. In units where there was great dissatisfaction with these appointed leaders, "work teams" were sent in from higher echelons to solicit ordinary people's opinions of who was best qualified for leadership. New leaders were often appointed in response to members' expressions of preference.

The time each person spent each week in political study meetings had decreased, and these meetings emphasized ideology far less than they had in the past; the time was devoted instead to practical matters such as bonuses and salaries. As a consequence, much of the earlier hatred of political study had dissipated. "Criticism/self-criticism" sessions and other compulsory rituals that forced each person to express an opinion also occurred much less frequently, although they did still take place. True, anyone who applied to join the Communist Youth League or the party had to write "thought reports" avowing loyalty to the party. However, in the spirit of the reforms, such "thought reports" could criticize the party's past mistakes and express the desire to help rectify the party's image. Since many of those who read the reports were likely to have been victims themselves at one time or another, they were often inclined to look favorably on outspoken criticism about past wrongs.

In the schools, there was still talk of the virtues of "political thought work," and all students were still required to take classes in politics, but the curriculum as a whole now focused on practical knowledge, not on ideology. The atmosphere in the most sophisticated urban schools was one of intense study for the middle school and highly selective university entrance examinations. Many families hired private tutors for their children, or arranged special summer classes. In the past, students honored as "Three Good" students (good morals, good grades, good health) were often those who spied on other students for the teachers. This practice was in early 1985 actively discouraged by teachers dismayed to have seen the heavily ideological education system transform children into little automatons. The 1984 film *The Girl in the Red Clothes* suggests that a sociable girl who pays attention to her personal appearance need not be disqualified as a "Three Good" student. (The film won the Golden Rooster award for the best Chinese film of the year.)

The attitude toward the West in the educational curriculum had shifted gradually from hostility or ignoring the West altogether to a cautious "introducing" of the subject.

Students were taught that China could "learn from" the West in matters of efficiency and productivity.

Because the reforms meant greater flexibility in finding jobs, the threat to students, teachers, and others of leaders' evaluations of their "thought" was far less powerful than in the past. If party leaders could not control individuals' destinies by evaluating their "political performance," it became irrelevant whether individuals believed in Marxism-Leninism or not.

Still, few were so foolish as to advertise their lack of belief in the virtues of the socialist system itself. Resistance to the reformers' policies of economic flexibility and the open door to the West had not ceased, so it was reasonable for people to fear a return to leftist policies and to wonder whether they would be penalized tomorrow for what it seemed safe to say and do today. A mood of caution continued to prevail, a care in dealing with others, a reluctance to have too many social contacts, a discrepancy between what was said at the office and what was said at home. Many believed that "it's not smart to be smart," complaining ironically that the really intelligent person mastered the art of self-preservation, which included maintaining good relations with superiors and appearing to lack curiosity about anything beyond one's own affairs. New parents sometimes agonized over how to educate their children, often deciding in favor of teaching them the obedience and industriousness that would give them safer lives. An entire generation of older intellectuals had been so intimidated and buffeted by political movements that they were content with political stability, freedom from movements, and an improving standard of living. They worried above all about bringing trouble upon themselves by any unorthodox behavior or unwelcome initiative; their fear of chaos was at least as powerful as their desire for more democracy. Most avoided direct conflict with the Four Basic Principles. Intelligent people who wished to criticize the party and its mistakes often cloaked their words in "the flag of reform": party policy encouraged criticism of the bureaucracy, of injustices toward intellectuals, and of abuses of power by party leaders. Others avoided discussing politics altogether, talking instead about life-style questions such as the price and quality of food and consumer goods.

Most intellectuals, still getting used to the radical improvement in their position, were deeply grateful that they were no longer among the most vilified of social groups. However, many dissidents, including some of the most distinguished democratic thinkers and editors of the short-lived "unofficial" magazines, had not yet been released from labor camps. There were few visible dissident activities in 1985; indeed, many former dissidents who were not incarcerated were supporting the reforms and some had entered the power structure as party members or even as party leaders. One former leader of the autumn 1980 democratic election movement sought us out, but it turned out that it was not to talk of democracy or human rights but to ask us to find foreign investors for a company he had set up to build a small museum and hotel. Another was said to be a housing official in the Special Economic Zone of Shenzhen. Many of these people would have preferred to see a more democratic China immediately, but had come to believe that the process would be more gradual than they once thought.

In early 1985 there were, however, occasional public demonstrations of protest, far more than those reported in the Western press. These were often merely small-scale expressions of disobedience. One group of peasants with whom we spoke near Xian was about to begin a sit-in on a piece of their land that they had turned into a profitable parking lot. Local officials, envious of their success, were trying to take over the land to set up a peasant market. In Hunan, so convinced were a number of families that housing in a newly constructed building would be unfairly allotted to officials and their friends that they broke into the apartments and moved in. They left finally, but not until assurances had been given that their claims would be given fair consideration.

A more conspicuous example of civil disobedience was the demonstrations at Beijing's city hall held in April 1985 by city dwellers who had been assigned to the countryside in Shanxi Province during the Cultural Revolution. It had been official policy that spouses living together could not return to the overcrowded cities they had come from (their "households" were considered complete, whereas an unmarried person's household was considered to be with his parents). Hundreds of thousands, perhaps millions, of Chinese did not therefore live in places they considered home. After the April demonstrations, a handful of people in Shanxi were allowed to return to Beijing, but countless others were still prevented from going home.

Many people arrested during the autumn 1983 campaign against spiritual pollution for involvement in "pornography" (the showing of "yellow" videotapes, participation in sexy dancing parties, distribution of pictures and books depicting sexual activities) remained in prison, but the sentences of some of the dissidents who expressed public criticism during the period of the Democracy Wall had been shortened. When we asked about Wei Jingsheng, China's most famous dissident, we were told that he was reading and writing his opinions on the reforms in a labor camp in Qinghai Province; he was not forced to do hard labor. Our sources, apparently reliable ones, who asked us not to reveal their names, gave us the impression in April 1985 that although some officials in the central government wanted him released, Public Security Bureau authorities stood in their way.

In 1985, few individuals were being arrested for political offenses. Most new prisoners were, rather, ordinary criminals, such as thieves, rapists, and murderers. These were the people whose rights were being violated most conspicuously, many of them executed without benefit of appeal, even for minor crimes such as stealing wristwatches. China's system of justice often operates on the principle of "killing the chicken to scare the monkey." In the apparent belief that everyone will enjoy a safer holiday if a firm warning is issued, a number of prisoners have been shot before major festivities each year. Mass pre-execution rallies have been held, with tickets distributed among members of the principal local work units and posters describing the cases displayed throughout the cities. Large red check marks are painted beside the names of offenders who have been dispatched. (In early 1986, yet another anti-crime campaign took place.)

For most people, however, life in early 1985 China seemed golden by comparison with the past. They could discuss "that short guy Deng," when once they could have been killed for referring to Chairman Mao as a "baldy." The reforms had given them opportunities to participate in political and economic life; their own primary concern was with bettering their standard of living, with the prices of goods, with procuring better clothing, food, and furniture. They seemed grateful for freedom to enjoy greater material comforts and for freedom from mass political campaigns, and seemed not to chafe because they could not exercise more direct control over their destinies.

Those intellectuals who would have liked to see China

even more free realized that the party had probably gone as far as it would go, at least for the time being, in liberalizing controls on speech and belief. To relax them much further could have put its position as ruling party in jeopardy, and possibly stimulate revolt against all reform by more orthodox party forces. Chinese people had grown accustomed to dealing with contradictory messages and sudden policy changes. On the one hand, they were urged to have the courage to use the greater economic autonomy being offered to them, and to find their own ways of making enterprises financially viable. On the other hand, when the implementation of these freedoms led to social tendencies of which party hard-liners disapproved, ideological work began and the political atmosphere grew cold. Such shifts were an accepted constant of Chinese life.

The Press

In early 1985, many journalists expressed pride to us in the increased circulation of their papers. Specialized publications such as *Peasant Journal, Peasant Evening News, Market Journal, Economic News,* and *Agronomy and Technology* had become lifelines in the countryside. In Sichuan's wealthy Wenjiang County, we learned that many peasants received seven or eight newspapers every day; there were reports of peasants in other parts of China who subscribed literally to hundreds. In the cities as well, newspapers and magazines were flourishing. Many local entrepreneurs had set up small street counters to sell magazines, books, and journals. A magazine shop worker in Chengdu told us that China published more than five thousand literary magazines. "Small newspapers," on every subject from fashion to sensational-

istic crime tales and kung fu stories, had popped up every-
where, despite dismayed orthodox party leaders' attempts
to close them down as "unhealthy." Much of this junk fare
for popular consumption was issued by traditional publishing houses and newspapers whose official products didn't
sell. As part of their attempt to show profitability and pay
good bonuses to their workers, they had turned to these
more marketable products.

Nevertheless, editors and journalists who would have
preferred to enliven the official media enjoyed only limited
freedom to do so. The freedom extended to writers and
artists during the writers' conference of late 1984–early 1985
was explicitly denied to them. In the April 14, 1985, *People's
Daily* a speech appeared by General Party Secretary Hu Yaobang, believed by some in the West to be a liberal reformer.
It showed where Hu really stood:

The party's news is the voice of the party, and naturally also the
voice of the people's government led by the party, and at the same
time the voice of the people themselves. . . . Some young comrades new to work and lacking in basic training perhaps do not
yet understand this basic point of view. . . .

Recently, after discussion, everyone feels the arts must enjoy
full creative freedom. Can news work also be conducted according
to the same slogan? I think it is not so simple. Of course, our
news work and art work should both enjoy the powers of freedom
given to them by the socialist system and the constitution . . . but
the party's news organs should represent the party and government, not only the editors and journalists themselves. . . .

Is it good that the news profession be the voice of the party
and government? Is it glorious? I think one must answer clearly:
"Very, very good. Very, very glorious." . . . To speak for the party,
how could it not be glorious? Only those very advanced in politics
and thought are capable of it. . . .

As for the question of different points of view, it depends on
which kind of question they are about. If they are on the country's
political direction or basic policies, as I said above, our people's

basic interests are one; the Central Committee and State Department's political direction and basic policies represent the interest of the people, so on these basic questions the unity of everyone's voice is necessary and natural, and to express "different" voices would be unnatural. . . .

I have heard there is a certain opinion that there is more democracy in capitalist countries, that their political system is better than ours. Everyone knows that capitalist countries are governed by people representing the interests of a minority of oppressors. Our country is managed by the majority of the people and their representatives. . . .

Young journalists from Shanxi Province expressed to us doubt that they would ever enjoy the most basic freedoms. When we described to them the high status of Western investigative journalists, and the monitoring function of the Western media over government, they listened with envy. The more local their newspapers, the more unfree, they said. One very articulate correspondent described some of the abuses by local officials he had uncovered. His decision not to write about these abuses had caused him much anguish, he said, but he knew that if he did write, only trouble would result.

In 1985 we also heard several tales of harassment of journalists. In Hunan, for example, a reporter from the local television station tried to investigate charges that the local commerce bureau was unfairly interfering with a private businessman, claiming that his new wealth was based on "smuggling." The journalist was convinced that this was a typical case of leftist ideology clashing with the reforms. Commerce bureau leaders refused to talk to him. In the past, without the cooperation of officials, that would have been the end of the matter, but the journalist persisted, and the bureau, in response, proceeded to send someone to tail him; he also received threatening telephone calls and letters. Eventually, national newspapers reported on the commerce bureau's behavior, citing the case as an example of the need for legal protections for journalists.

An even more notorious incident occurred in Beijing in early 1985, when a *Beijing Evening News* reporter who was attending an exhibition called a taxi for a woman who had fainted. The guards at the exhibition hall refused to open the metal gate to allow the car in, although the sick woman lay in plain view; they cited lack of permission from their leaders. Enraged, the journalist took out his camera to photograph the unconscious woman, the waiting taxi, and the locked gate. The guards grabbed him, seized his film, beat him, and tore up the press identification he had produced. In the confusion, bystanders carried the woman through a side door to the waiting taxi, and the journalist was lauded for having suffered persecution in a humanitarian cause.

Despite such restrictions on journalists, access to knowledge of the outside was continuing to increase in China, a trend demonstrated by statistics on academic exchange, on travel abroad, translations of foreign works, and television broadcasting of foreign news and features. The openness was brought home to us most clearly when, in an exceedingly poor county town during the days before Spring Festival, we were unable to find a Chinese movie among the American and European films and the Hong Kong kung fu videotapes, which were said to be becoming a threat to the Chinese film industry. Foreign films were no longer chosen, as they had been some years earlier, for their negative pictures of the West and capitalist society; these were films of love, crime, intrigue, and adventure.

The Economic Reforms and Artistic Freedom

The conclusion of the campaign against spiritual pollution gave writers and artists new hope. This, plus the urban economic and systemic reforms which affected arts units and associations, created an atmosphere of comparatively great artistic freedom. Writers and artists previously unable to accept fees for lectures, instruction, or independent sales of art works, and rewarded, if at all, with safe gifts of food or small souvenirs, could now receive payments. Many music teachers were now paid to give private lessons; painters could sell their work, on the streets if they liked; and famous writers, artists, and intellectuals could negotiate honoraria for speeches. Writers of articles no longer had to go first to their leaders to have them "approved," but could send them directly to any publication; some courageous ones even submitted pieces to magazines outside China.

The question of payment for services was of great importance to China's artists, perhaps even more so than the question of creative freedom itself. One of their greatest complaints involved precisely this matter: as members of "professional units" rather than "enterprises," they were permitted to receive money only from activities directly connected with their occupations. Because what most of them did had little or no market value, they often felt that workers and peasants had much more freedom to take advantage of the new economic policies than they. Although there was always a back door in China for the famous and well-connected, the rules for most artists were strict. There were even stories of actors being arrested for doing business.

Within their spheres, however, a small number of artists had become financially quite successful. The greatest money-makers in early 1985 were singers of "light music" (pop songs) and teachers of disco dancing, although in November, when the atmosphere tightened, one popular male singer, Zhang Xing, was prohibited from making cassettes or performing in public, and some speculated that this was because of jealousy of his high earnings.[1] Some respected artists with clout had formed private troupes in the freer Special Economic Zones (where only a limited number of influential or highly qualified people from the interior were permitted to live). For example, in Shenzhen a privately run dance troupe and a film company which sought to work with foreigners had been established. Other artists enjoyed the freedom to form temporary troupes for individual projects, or even to be hired, as were some film artists and technicians, by Hong Kong movie makers. New flexibilities allowed artists to withdraw temporarily from their work units, sacrificing their salaries but not their affiliations, to find work elsewhere.

The economic reforms had altered the leadership of the arts units and associations. Party functions were being separated from troupe or studio functions, giving relatively more knowledgeable and often freely elected leaders greater artistic control. Fewer layers of permission and of revision of the original conception of a work were generally necessary, and such approvals were granted by officials with background in the field rather than by those with none. Under this more reasonable leadership, most artists felt more comfortable than they had under the control of party bureaucrats who had not the faintest understanding of their discipline.

However, in liberal as in repressive times, people still complained that new leaders were often, in effect, quite similar to the old ones. Troupe leaders anxious to hold on to talent could still easily stop the transfer of a highly successful artist who felt stifled in one unit and had a better offer elsewhere. If he wished to withdraw temporarily, sacrificing a guaranteed salary, the leaders had little power to say no, but their power over permanent transfers was another matter. Young artists accepted at professional arts institutes were often prevented from attending by leaders who claimed they were needed at home. As in the past, there was no appeal of such decisions. The greater mobility had thus affected relatively few artists. Most had little opportunity for other work, lacking the means and connections to strike out on their own, or simply too accustomed to "the iron rice bowl" to dare to risk a more independent and unpredictable professional life. The economic reforms thus seemed all but irrelevant to many people in the arts.

If the changes in economic structure had not fundamentally altered the daily lives of most writers and artists, the Writers' Conference, which was held for eight days in December 1984–January 1985, was a subject of deep concern to all of them. It marked the party's most liberal stance toward the arts since before Mao's 1942 "Talks at the Yanan Forum on Literature and Art."

Even before we arrived in China in early 1985, the fame of the conference had spread to the outside world, with its major theme the party's promise that there would be no more interference in the arts. Some months earlier, Central Committee leader Wan Li, in an "internal speech," had criticized the party for failing to understand art and even for neglecting economics. This set the stage for the liberal mood. The first striking sign of a change in tone came in the issuance of new invitations to the Writers' Conference. The lists of participants had initially been selected not long after the campaign against spiritual pollution, and naturally the names of many of the most outspoken writers were conspicuously absent. However, all the public attention had served only to strengthen the literary reputations of those criticized, and sentiment ran strong that these writers should be invited to the Writers' Conference. Honorary invitations to several named as specific targets of the campaign against spiritual pollution were issued.

Young Secretary Hu Qili represented the Secretariat in delivering the conference's opening address, and his remarks sounded very sweet indeed. Here are some excerpts:[2]

Literary creation is a spiritual labor. The results of the work have the writer's clearly individual characteristics. It is necessary to give free rein to individual creativity, powers of observation, and imagination. It is necessary to have a deep understanding and unique opinions of life, as well as unique artistic techniques. The writer must think for himself, have full freedom to choose subjects, themes, and methods of artistic expression, to have full freedom to express his own feelings, excitement, and thought. . . .

For a long time, the party has interfered too much, given too many "labels," too many administrative orders. The cadres sent by the party to the literature and art associations are good comrades, but they don't understand much about literature and art, and have harmed the relationship between the party and literature and art workers. . . .

As for the shortcomings and problems occurring in the course of literary creation, as long as no laws are broken, they should be resolved only through criticism, discussion, and debate among literary critics. The writers criticized should not be discriminated against politically, and should not be mistreated by their organizations. . . .

This keynote gave writers the courage to speak of what was uppermost in their hearts and minds: their hatred and fear of leftist persecution. According to the published diary of Liu Binyan, the famous "exposé literature" writer, the condemnation of leftism was one of the main themes of the conference. As quoted by Liu, one famous writer, Lu Wenfu, said:[3]

People opposing the right have many methods, "forcing opinions," "creating discussion," "holding big criticisms," "collecting materials," "dealing with people through the 'organization.'" Of course, we should not use these reprehensible methods to oppose the Left. But how can we do it? Writers should think about this.

And a poet said:

In published opinions, a bit of leftism isn't so frightening. But if leaders themselves are leftist, it can mean death for some writers. Therefore, when leftism and power are linked together, it is very dangerous.

People's Daily art page director Yuan Ying's complaints appeared in an article printed before the meeting:[4]

In literature and art, the history of leftism is long and deep, the damage great . . . it has reached the point that although the Gang of Four was smashed eight years ago, there has still been no strong and clear criticism of leftist thought. There has even been a strange phenomenon: in the economy, leftism is opposed, but in literature and art, rightism is. This is not logical, practical, or defensible.

The opening session of the Writers' Conference gave further evidence of writers' feelings about the spiritual pollution campaign. A number of unpopular leaders were absent from the conference, with excuses of illness. Propaganda Chief Deng Liqun, chief architect of the 1983 movement, and Hu Qiaomu, Central Committee Political Department member in charge of ideology, did not come. Nor did rehabilitated party theorist Zhou Yang, one of the 1983 campaign's main targets because of his discussions of socialist alienation and "developed" Marxism, who was in genuinely poor health.

When the messages of congratulations from the absent leaders were conveyed, the audience of writers reacted politely. But when Zhou Yang's words were read, there was thunderous applause for a full five minutes, and some reported they were moved to tears.

Even more interesting to some than the speeches was the quiet rebellion behind the scenes by writers from various provinces against the people their local propaganda departments had selected as candidates for election to the Writers' Council. The writers' associations were supposed to be organizations for the masses, for ordinary people, writers complained. They should be like clubs, not big party-controlled bureaucracies which existed to control and criticize their members. It was wrong that so many of the officers were party-selected ideologues who did not reflect the writers' interests.

Each province handled the matter differently, some adding candidates, others selecting anew. Hu Qili's speech about artistic freedom had thus added a corollary freedom: that of increased political participation. The results were radical, and quite embarrassing for the official arts bureaucracy. Many of the perennial party favorites were not reelected, or, like the political fence-sitter Ding Ling, made it by a shamefully low margin. Fifty-eight percent of the newly elected council members had never served before, and 38 percent were under the age of fifty-five, thus drastically rejuvenating the group. Similar changes were made among the thirty-two directors of the conference, 40 percent of whom were below the age of sixty, one only thirty-two, a callow youth who under ordinary circumstances could not have seen a leadership position for many more years. About half of the directors were known for their free thinking, and many of them were ex-rightists. He Jingzhi, one of the supporters of the campaign against spiritual pollution, and party Central Committee member as well as ex–vice chairman of the Writers' Association, lost his power; the old novelist Ba Jin, popular for his outspokenness against party interference in the arts, became the new chairman.

The meeting was short, but its impact was great on artists throughout China in every field, and even on journalists who, following the conference, began to discuss the need for legal guarantees of freedom of the press. The generally positive mood among other intellectuals with whom we spoke in early 1985 had much to do with the heady atmosphere of the meeting.

Many writers, however, were skeptical about whether the party would make good its promises, and for good reason. The conservative arts officials and writers present at the December-to-January conference remained conspicuously silent throughout, as if biding their time; some writers wondered why these officers were not forced to give their opinions, as they themselves had been forced to do about leftist policies in so many earlier meetings. A more important reason for most writers' hesitations, however, was their long history of persecutions and their expectations of sharp shifts in the political winds. None of them would have been so naive as to think that artistic freedom under the Communist party meant they had the freedom to speak against the party and against socialism. Others pointed out that freedom "given" from above can just as easily be taken away.

The respected novelist Wu Zuguang had told the meeting that his wife, who had been persecuted because he had been labeled a "rightist" following remarks he made in 1957, had read and modified his draft.[5] She had threatened to get up in the assembly and prevent him from continuing if he was too truthful. A noted actress, she had once been ordered by the minister of culture to divorce her husband, but had refused. Too famous to be denied the right to perform, offstage she had been humiliated and sent to clean outhouses.

After seven years of digging air-raid shelters, she had had a stroke and lost the use of one of her hands.

Wu Zuguang said he had been in the United States during the campaign against spiritual pollution. He spoke out against it, and when he went home, the Ministry of Culture criticized him for opposing the party and threatened to arrest him. If the party could treat writers like this, Wu said, why should leftists sitting in the audience be free of fear for their own safety?

The cautious attitude of Wu and others was well founded. Publicity about the conference was limited. In comparison with the conference of 1979, there was little coverage of this one, only two articles in the *People's Daily*. This media silence reflected, many felt, the displeasure of the Propaganda Ministry, which controlled the news organizations. It was a sign of the strength of those unhappy about the party's promises, and of their determination not to allow the whole society to join the discussion of intellectual freedom. Then in the April 14, 1985, speech on journalism, several months after the conference, Party Secretary Hu Yaobang offered a far more conservative interpretation of artistic freedom than that offered by Secretary Hu Qili:

The social function of artists . . . is, through their art, to inspire and educate the people, to exert a subtle influence on their souls. This function, in the words frequently quoted by Comrade [Deng] Xiaoping, is precisely to be "engineers of the souls of the people." The party's writers will express the party's nature and support the party's line, direction, and policies, and will also convey the voice of the party in their works. But the party should never tell this or that writer what to write. . . . Only then can be written works truly affecting, truly of educational value. . . .

Winds continued to cool over the course of the year, growing coldest in autumn. During the September meeting of the Central Committee, Deng Xiaoping managed to force 64 senior orthodox party officials out of a total of 340 to retire.[6] In order to realize this political victory, however, he made concessions to hard-liners by an increased emphasis on ideology. Deng had shown himself fully capable of casting his weight with forces of repression or liberalization as it suited his own main goal, to make China a strong, modern world power. An additional impetus to increased tightness had been some of the problems with the urban economic reforms: the spring of 1985 had seen an attack on tax evasion and on abuses of economic freedoms by managers issuing bonuses that exceeded their enterprises' means to the workers who had elected them; the summer had seen the exposure of some of the most widespread corruption scandals in China's recent history, especially that of Hainan Island officials taking advantage of Hainan's new status as a Special Economic Zone to import expensive, hard-to-get goods like automobiles and color television sets, engaging in black market foreign currency exchange scams to do so, and reselling them to people in the interior of the country at huge profits. Even the *Hainan Daily* (*Hainan Ribao*) went into the car trade, and it cost the chief editor his job.[7]

As the pace of the economic reforms slowed in response, ideological work increased. The September issue of *Democracy and Law* (*Minzhu yu Fazhi*), for example, revived criticisms of "looking toward money in everything." In autumn 1985 in literature and the arts, there were criticisms of certain works, although the criticisms could hardly be said to constitute a campaign of the strength of that against bourgeois liberalism of 1981 or that against spiritual pollution of 1983. The works under fire included a play, *We* (*WM*, for *Women*, in Chinese),[8] about seven teenagers sent down to the countryside during the Cultural Revolution; "The Second Loyalty" (*Dier zhong Zhongcheng*),[9] a piece of reportage literature by Liu Binyan, the courageous exposé writer who was elected to the post of vice-chairman of the Writers' Association during the 1984–1985 Writers' Conference; and a novella by Zhang Xianliang, *Half of a Man Is Woman* (*Nanren de Yiban shi Nuren*).[10]

The play, which was closed first in Beijing and then in Shanghai when it moved there, portrays China's youth as living in an unjust society fraught with ills; in a subject reminiscent of the controversial play by Sha Yexin, *If I Were Real*, the son of a high-ranking official rises far faster than those who do not have his connections.

It looked as if Liu Binyan were in trouble when with the June issue *Wenhui Magazine* (*Wenhui Zazhi*) suddenly stopped printing its serialization of a highly critical and penetrating diary he kept during the 1984–1985 Writers' Conference. Then "The Second Loyalty," which tells of the persecution of two party members during the Cultural Revolution, was criticized. In the piece, the party members are loyal to their own vision of an upstanding party, to their ideas of truth. (The "first loyalty" is the kind of self-sacrificing but mechanistic loyalty of a Lei Feng, the model soldier of the Mao era.) The criticisms of this work were complex: on the one hand, it could be argued that it was Liu's advocacy of free speech that was being attacked; however, another problem was that Liu's outspoken party members were advocating better relations with the Soviet Union, a politically sensitive subject in 1985 as it was during the 1960s, when the story is set.

The problem with Zhang Xianliang's work was said to be that it was depraved, dealing too explicitly with sex. It describes two Cultural Revolution victims who lose their sexual functions during their prison years, only to rediscover them through marriage to each other in better times. This study of sexual psychology was said to have potential corrupting effects on the young, leading them to commit crimes.

Other signs of the tighter climate were a November writers' workshop in which officials called on writers to exercise more self-restraint and treat themes that "serve socialism."[11] New regulations governing the use of paper and the registration of magazines forced most "small newspapers" to close. At the same time, filmmakers were urged to consider more seriously the social effects of their work. A major anticrime campaign, always a sign of increasing social controls, got under way toward the beginning of 1986. Furthermore, an influential article in the December 1985 issue of *Red Flag*, the party's theoretical journal, criticized the anti-Japanese student demonstrations of previous months as regressions to the "Four Greats" of Cultural Revolution–style politics. It also attacked writers for being excessively individualistic, saying that when people in China use freedom, they should first think of how it can be used in the service of the people and socialism. While rejecting the Ultraleft, the article also criticized bourgeois liberalism and capitalist corruption.

Such trends indicate that the familiar tale of fluctuations between tightness and looseness continues. The outcome of this latest chapter is yet to be told. Yet perhaps it will not be such a terrifying story. Writers, artists, and intellectuals are rarely surprised by such shifts. They have learned to take their blessings where they find them, living patiently, cautiously, and self-protectively, the astutest weather-watchers of them all.

In early 1985, just after the Writers' Conference, several writers told us that their comparative new freedom had presented them with a new challenge, simply as artists. For the first time in recent memory, they had to struggle not primarily against political restrictions on subject matter and literary technique but within themselves, to find out whether, after all these years, they could produce world-class literature.

World recognition was terribly important to them, for they acutely recognized that China had published no work of international stature since the 1930s. China's intense national pride, born of centuries of greatness, made their current backwardness and inadequacy especially painful to them. Many of China's artists and writers said they worried about why China had not produced great contemporary art. After years of being trained as the party's tools for instilling socialist morality and stirring the masses to enthusiasm for socialist construction, they wondered whether they were capable of anything but routine small adventures into forbidden zones. They traced the problem not only to their internalization of socialist restrictions, but, because they knew that the Soviet Union's and Eastern Europe's literary worlds were flourishing, to aspects of Chinese national character such as passivity and the noncombative relationship of Chinese intellectuals to authority. They pointed out that for thousands of years intellectuals and policy makers had had a close relationship in which intellectuals saw themselves primarily as constructive critics, helping the emperor and his officials to carry out the Confucian ideal of the paternal ruler who treats his subjects as his family.

Writers with whom we spoke from the younger generation saw themselves as quite different from their elders. They said that most of the older writers had been so beaten down by political movements that it was too late for them; they saw the middle-aged generation of ex-rightists, while often courageous, as seeking only the freedom to criticize the darker aspects of society, while remaining strongly in the socialist realist tradition in which it had been trained.

They believed that this middle generation was still committed to black and white choices and two-dimensional characters; that their literature was primarily political, and intimately entwined with social and moral judgments, no matter how much they spoke of literary expression.

Younger writers, on the other hand, expressed interest in tapping China's folk roots; some said they made expeditions into China's backwaters, to speak to old sorcerers and collect ancient legends. They hoped to draw on China's primitive traditions as well as on modern Western literary techniques, and were particularly interested in looking to South American writers for inspiration. They rejected the simplistic characters and easy value judgments of China's recent literature, believing that if they did so, China would be able to produce great and uniquely Chinese work within the next ten years. If the recent "tightness" proves insignificant, there is an excellent chance that they are right. In the availability of raw material, literary sensibility, and richness of language, China provides all the conditions for many masterpieces. At the very least, those who remain within the critical realist tradition should be able to produce a great work set during the Cultural Revolution. At the same time, China's unprecedented openness to translations of foreign literature, and the resurgence of teaching of foreign languages, should help China's new young writers move quickly into the world community.

Epilogue

Despite the recent tightening of late 1985 and early 1986, China may be, in some respects, at its most free since the pre-1949 years. Personal and artistic freedoms and human rights are still very limited by Western criteria, but in comparison with the fascist repressions of the still-recent decade of the 1966–1976 Cultural Revolution, the "warmer" climate is remarkable.

Even the liberal Hundred Flowers Campaign of 1956 cannot match the warm winds of today in terms of access to Western ideas and to the outside world. The Democracy Wall Movement of 1978–1979 brought more public outcry than the quieter freedom of the mid-1980s, but many of the injustices that caused the bold protests of those earlier years—mistreatment of intellectuals, party corruption, indifferent political participation—have been slowly remedied. Many of the activists who have recently been released from labor camps and many who were never arrested have brought influence to bear in support of economic reforms, for they believe that only a stronger economic foundation can support a more democratic political structure and up-root entrenched feudal traditions such as blind obedience to authority, and government by personal connections rather than law.

This older generation is often frightened by some of their now-adult children, the so-called "lost generation" of

China, who heard socialist promises from childhood and experienced instead tragedy, loss of education, and disillusionment. These young people, now about thirty to forty-five, have no memories of beggars and famines before 1949 to ease their sense of betrayal. The Cultural Revolution came when their expectations were highest and they were at their most impressionable; their unusual experiences, from the free train rides they were allowed to take in order to spread "revolution," to their hard lives as "educated youths" in the countryside, gave them a deep understanding of Chinese society and a concern for its problems. They are now more vigorous and willing to take risks than are their broken and exhausted parents. Many of them have been open about their disillusionment with socialism, or at least with the Chinese version, which created a new class of exploiters, corrupt and uneducated party bureaucrats who repeated ideology and slogans but whose privileged life styles mocked them. The greatest push for freedom of expression has been among these young people. They have welcomed opportunities to denounce the hypocrisy around them, to discover a way to help China, and to find something in which to believe. That something has often turned out to be the power of the individual; hence their frequent interest in existentialism, Christianity, and humanism, all of which are quite incompatible with socialist orthodoxy.

The young people's thirst for intellectual freedom led them in the late seventies to overstep the more liberal bounds set by the Deng reformers, and, as in the campaign of 1983, they have at times been reined in very tightly. Since they comprise a large part of the urban work force, they continue to pose a great challenge to the party, which is increasingly concerned about the "inheritors of the revolution." If the Deng regime is successful in restoring the party's integrity by bringing in younger, better educated members, and is able, at the same time, to keep up with people's rising material expectations through the economic reforms, the crisis of confidence is likely eventually to be resolved. As the younger generation moves into positions of power, their attitudes and beliefs will determine the future of Chinese socialism.

Even if the problem of the young can be solved, urban reforms will not be easy. The entrenched local bureaucracy distorts the spirit of new policies; uneducated leftists and the Soviet faction wait for the reformers to make fatal mistakes; almost everything is still accomplished through under-the-table deals. Inadequate accounting procedures, inflation, and lack of social security and unemployment systems have recently intensified problems. Reformers are clear about the failures of Soviet-style centrally planned production; they are less clear about what China's own course should be, describing themselves as "groping for stepping stones while crossing the river."

To them, economic reform is a vehicle for the fundamental reorganization of China's political, intellectual, social, and cultural life. Although it is far from certain that they will succeed, their vision for the future seems to include a democratization of the party that would soften its autocratic nature; such a revision of the party's role and scope of its power has already begun, with great consequences for intellectual freedom.

The tragedy of the Cultural Revolution has put China in a very different position from, say, the Soviet Union during its period of economic reform. The Chinese people have learned terrible lessons about the dangers of political campaigns and anti-intellectualism, and these will not easily be forgotten. With each passing year of openness to the West and internal liberalization, the chances that Stalin-scale purges may recur in China appear increasingly remote.

China is now in a race for time: Deng Xiaoping, in 1986 already eighty-two, has said he expects to live until he is eighty-five. If the economic situation worsens, and Maoists within the party are able to muster their forces as they have been attempting to do once again in autumn 1985, there is a danger that the comparatively "warm" weather in China now could once again pass into deep winter. Deng's task is not easy. During the time remaining to him, he must protect his modernization program against its opponents, improve the party's image, control the corruption of those who seek to take advantage of the reforms for personal gain and contain the resentment of those who see others as benefiting from them more than they, as well as solve the many new problems that the reforms have created so as to prove that socialism can bring the people a reasonably good standard of living.

Increased Sino-Western contact could be crucial to the continuation of the reforms after his death. Many reformers firmly believe that certain aspects of Western values and culture hold the key to the release of China from its cycle of feudalistic politics of personality. The more dealings China has with the West and the more stable its economic policies, the greater will be the number of Chinese who have some understanding of Western society and are unwilling to return to an emphasis on ideological orthodoxy and class struggle. These people will be China's hope that the xenophobic Maoist radicals and those conservatives who are nostalgic for the pro-Soviet 1950s will be unable to marshal a comeback after Deng's death. Still, the conflict between modern and feudal ideas will probably continue for many years; uneducated middle- and lower-level cadres who lack the ability to keep pace with new policies will remain reluctant to give up their power to more skilled professionals. China's young and many of its top leaders welcome change, but the forces resisting it must not be underestimated. Fluctuations between warm and cold winds can thus be expected to be a continuing feature of life in China. Yet, greater intellectual freedom, and certainly a greater thirst for such freedom, cannot help but accompany modernization and the new emphasis on education and skills. Political and economic stability, ironically, are the surest ways of bringing about change in China.

Although continued success for the economic reforms will not guarantee the eventual success of China's writers and artists, or the continuation or expansion of intellectual and personal freedom, it could well be a precondition. The fragile liberties now being explored cannot be separated from this extremely difficult experiment. We are optimistic about the future of intellectuals in China, but have a deep appreciation of the many pitfalls the reformers face. They once again may have to make quick sacrifices of personal and intellectual freedoms if there should be strong attacks from more orthodox leaders.

The climate of China often shifts with great suddenness; enormous transformations will again surely take place. China's Communist party has a history of some of the most fearsome totalitarianism of this century, and it could easily be revived. The tightening of recent months, with appeals once again to writers and filmmakers to "consider the social effects" of their work, and the anticrime campaign of early 1986, indicate that there will be continuous oscillations between liberal times such as that of early 1985 and periods of "increased political thought work" such as in late 1983. However, if China's leaders do not reverse the new and astonishingly original intellectual and personal freedoms, the story of China after the death of Mao could still be one of the most remarkable tales of liberation ever told.

Notes

All translations from Chinese sources are by the authors unless otherwise noted.

Key to Abbreviations

DXPWX	*Deng Xiaoping Wenxuan*	*Collected Works of Deng Xiaoping*
DYCZ	*Dianying Chuangzuo* (Beijing)	*Film Creation*
FBIS		Foreign Broadcast Information Service
GMRB	*Guangming Ribao* (Beijing)	*Guangming Daily*
NYT		*New York Times*
QSND	*Qishi Niandai* (Hong Kong)	*The Seventies*
RMRB	*Renmin Ribao* (Beijing)	*People's Daily*
RMWX	*Renmin Wenxue* (Beijing)	*People's Literature*
RMYY	*Renmin Yinyue* (Beijing)	*People's Music*
SH	*Shouhuo* (Beijing)	*Harvest*
SHWX	*Shanghai Wenxue* (Shanghai)	*Shanghai Literature*
SK	*Shikan* (Beijing)	*Poetry*
SY	*Shiyue* (Beijing)	*October*

WHB	*Wenhuibao* (Shanghai)	
WXB	*Wenxue Bao* (Shanghai)	*Literature Bulletin*
WYB	*Wenyi Bao* (Beijing)	*Literature and Art Bulletin*
XJB	*Xiju Bao* (Beijing)	*Drama Bulletin*
XWZX	*Xinwen Zhanxian* (Beijing)	*News Front*
ZGQN	*Zhongguo Qingnian* (Beijing)	*China Youth*
ZM	*Zhengming* (Hong Kong)	*Discussion*
ZPYZM	*Zuopin Yu Zhengming* (Beijing)	*Works and Discussion*

Prologue

1. See, for example, James D. Seymour, ed., *The Fifth Modernization* (New York: Earl Coleman, 1981), and David S. G. Goodman, *Beijing Street Voices* (New Hampshire: Marion Boyars, 1981).

A Golden Time

1. ZGQN, May 1980.
2. RMWX, September 1979.
3. QSND, January 1980.
4. SK, August 1979.
5. "Chinese Art After Mao," slide/tape module by the Center for International Studies, University of Pittsburgh, 1983.
6. Perry Link, *Stubborn Weeds* (Bloomington: Indiana University Press), p. 22.
7. RMWX, November 1977.
8. WHB, August 11, 1978.
9. RMWX, February 1980.
10. RMWX, July 1979.
11. SY, April 1981.
12. *Huaxi* (Guizhou), October 1980.
13. SY, January 1980.
14. SY, January 1981.

15. Dai Houying, *Ren, A Ren* (Guangdong: Huacheng Chubanshe, 1980).
16. SH, January 1980.
17. DYCZ, October 1979.
18. SHWX, September 1981. Here translated by W. J. F. Jenner in *Stubborn Weeds*, op. cit., p. 187.
19. *Xingxing* (Chengdu), March 1980. Here translated by William Tay in *Stubborn Weeds*, op. cit., p. 185.
20. SK, October 1980. Here translated by William Tay in *Stubborn Weeds*, op. cit., p. 185.
21. *Stubborn Weeds*, op. cit., p. 20.
22. Many important speeches from this congress have been translated in Howard Goldblatt, ed., *Chinese Literature for the 1980s* (Armonk, New York: M. E. Sharpe, 1982).
23. Ibid., pp. 7–14. WYB, November–December 1979.
24. Ibid., pp. 152–53.
25. Ibid., pp. 148–56.
26. Ibid., pp. 161–68.

A Darker Time

1. DXPWX, (Beijing: Renmin Chubanshe, 1983), pp. 344–48.

2. DYCZ, November 1979.
3. *Stubborn Weeds*, op. cit., p. 22.
4. DXPWX, op. cit., p. 313, p. 324.
See also, QSND, June 1981.
5. DXPWX, op. cit., p. 334.
6. DXPWX, op. cit., pp. 344–48.
7. RMRB, August 31, 1981. (Hu Yao-bang's "Speech at the Conference on National Thought Front Questions.")
8. *Stubborn Weeds*, op. cit., p. 15.
9. RMRB, December 30, 1981. (Hu Yaobang's "Speech to Representatives of the Feature Film Creators' Meeting.")

An Erratic Climate

1. RMRB, December 9, 1983.
2. NYT, November 18, 1983.
3. QSND, February 1983.
4. Department of State, *Country Report on Human Rights Practices for 1983* (Washington, D.C.: U.S. Government Printing Office, 1984), p. 743.

"Good" Thought and "Bad"

1. ZM, June 1983.
2. RMRB, November 28, 1983.
3. ZM, June 1983.
4. RMRB, September 1983.

Speech and Silence

1. DXPWX, op. cit., p. 221.
2. Conversation with Professor Andrew J. Nathan, Columbia University.
3. Department of State Report, op. cit., p. 745.

Political Participation and Protest

1. RMRB, March 3, 1984.
2. The work team method was used, for example, during the 1984 party rectification. See RMRB, December 21, 1983.

Religion and the Drive Against Superstition

1. Department of State Report, op. cit., p. 748.
2. *Inside China Mainland* (Taiwan) May 1983. (English translation of Document No. 19.)
3. The Department of State Report puts the figure at 15 million.
4. The Department of State Report says there are 20,000 mosques and 400 functioning churches.
5. *Inside China Mainland*, op. cit., p. 6.
6. Summarized ibid., p. 2.
7. *SpeaHRhead* (New York), No. 16, Northern Winter 1982–1983, p. 21 (from *Fujian Ribao*).
8. *Washington Post*, March 30, 1984.
9. GMRB, April 20, 1981.
10. *NewsTibet* (New York), September–December 1983. The Tibetans are a very special case among China's ethnic minorities, because Tibet was once a wholly independent country. It is beyond the scope of this book to treat the situation there in depth, but interested people may refer to this publication of the Dalai Lama's New York office, which monitors the human rights situation there.
11. *Inside China Mainland*, op. cit., p. 9.
12. Official Statement quoted in *Index on Censorship* (London), May 1983.
13. Department of State Report, op. cit., p. 749.
14. RMRB, December 16, 1983.

The Arts

1. Hunan materials based on personal interviews.
2. RMRB, January 7, 1983.
3. XJB, March 1983.
4. RMRB, February 6, 1983.
5. Hunan is not a dance-loving area, but the troupe's difficulty finding audiences was in part because of party

control of the contents of the performances the dancers had available.
6. ZPYZM, April 1983.
7. *Zhongguo zhi Chun* (*China Spring*), December 1983.
8. XJB, July 1983.
9. RMRB, August 4, 1983.
10. RMRB, October 14, 1983.
11. RMRB, December 3, 1983.
12. XJB, September 1983.
13. Howard Goldblatt, ed., *Chinese Literature for the 1980s* (Armonk, New York: M. E. Sharpe, 1982), p. xviii.
14. The works awarded prizes do, in fact, reflect these statements. See, for example, SK, June 1983.
15. *Zhongguo.Wenxue Yanjiu Nianjian* (Beijing: Zhongguo Shehui Kexue Chubanshe), "Speech at the Conference on Playwriting," p. 181.
16. *Beijing Review* (Beijing), October 17, 1983.
17. ZM, February 1984.
18. Ibid.
19. RMRB, October 31, 1983.
20. Hunan materials based on personal interviews.
21. FBIS, November 8, 1983.
22. RMRB, October 31, 1983.
23. Ibid.
24. RMRB, November 2, 1983.
25. RMRB, November 10, 1983.
26. ZM, December 1983.
27. SY, January 1981.
28. ZPSYZM, July 1983.
29. GMRB, November 8, 1983.
30. *Nanfang Ribao* (Guangzhou), November 7, 1983.
31. *Ren, A Ren*, op. cit., p. 351.
32. Ibid., p. 354.
33. *Xin Yuan* (Changchun), February 1982.
34. ZPYZM, June 1983.
35. Ibid.
36. *Jilin Ribao* (Changchun), February 19, 1983.
37. RMRB, November 1, 1983.
38. *Los Angeles Times*, February 19, 1982.
39. Ibid.
40. RMRB, November 5, 1983.
41. RMRB, December 23, 1983.

42. GMRB, May 5, 1980.
43. SK, March 1981.
44. *Dangdai Wenyi Sichao* (Lanzhou), January 1983.
45. WXB, November 3, 1983.
46. See, for example, SK, November 1983.
47. WYB, December 1983.
48. WYB, November 1983.
49. RMRB, October 28, 1983.
50. SHWX, May 1983. Also see WYB, November 1983.
51. SK, March 1979. For other criticisms, see *Beijing Wenyi* (Beijing), March 1983, *Keshi Women Xiangxin*, and SK, December 1983, *Zai Juequi Shenglang Qianmian*.
52. ZM, March 1984. See also *Jueqi de Shiqun: Zhongguo Dangdai Menglong Shi Yu Shilun Wenxue* (Hong Kong: *Dangdai Wenxue Yanjiu Shi*, February 1984).
53. RMRB, October 25, 1983.
54. RMRB, November 9, 1983.
55. RMRB, November 13, 1983.
56. RMRB, November 1, 1983.
57. See, for example, WYB, December 1983.
58. Personal interview with a member of the Philosophy Research Institute of the Chinese Academy of Social Sciences.
59. WYB, August 1983; September 1983.
60. WYB, October 1983.
61. FBIS, November 8, 1983.
62. RMRB, October 30, 1983.
63. WYB, June 1983.
64. WYB, November 1983.
65. RMYY, September 1983.
66. RMYY, September 1983.
67. WYB, November 1983.

The Press

1. *Zhongguo Chuban Nianjian* (Beijing: Shangwu Yinshuaguan, 1982), pp. 122–29.
2. Andrew J. Nathan, "Propaganda and Alienation in the People's Republic of China," draft chapter for *Chinese Democracy* (New York: Knopf, 1985).

3. Ibid.
4. RMRB, December 13, 1983. See also XWZX, February 1984.
5. Nathan, op. cit.
6. Ibid. Hu was demoted (in an apparent promotion) to the post of director from that of chief editor in May 1982.
7. XWZX, April 1983.
8. XWZX, July 1983.
9. XWZX, August 1983.
10. RMRB, March 12, 1983.
11. Agence France-Presse, November 13, 1983; December 1983.
12. RMRB, December 12, 1983.
13. NYT, April 18, 1984, p. C29.
14. XWZX, May 1983.
15. XWZX, August 1983.
16. RMRB, November 21, 1983.
17. RMRB, December 1, 1983.
18. *Zhongguo Chuban Nianjian*, op. cit.
19. RMRB, January 9, 1983.
20. RMRB, March 17, 1983.
21. RMRB, December 3, 1983.

The End of the Campaign Against Spiritual Pollution

1. RMRB, October 13, 1983.
2. ZM, February 1984. The description of the report echoes numerous subsequently published articles.
3. RMRB, December 9, 1983.
4. RMRB, December 10, 1983.
5. RMRB, December 16, 1983.
6. RMRB, December 18, 1983.
7. *Huayu Kuaibao* (New York), December 21, 1983.
8. RMRB, December 21, 1983.

The Economic Reforms and Artistic Freedom

1. *Washington Post*, November 22, 1985.
2. See, for example, *Zhongguo Xinwen*, December 1984.
3. *Wenhui Yuekan*, February 1985.
4. QSND, February 1985.
5. ZM, March 1985.
6. NYT, September 18, 1985.
7. NYT, December 13, 1985.
8. ZM, December 1985.
9. ZM, October 1985.
10. ZM, November 1985.
11. See, for example, *Huaqiao Ribao* (New York), November 2, 1985.

Index